BLAGGERS INC.
BRITAIN'S BIGGEST
ARMED ROBBERIES

By the same author:

The Art of Armed Robbery (John Blake Publishing, 2003)
Two Strikes and You're Out! (Able Publishing, 2005)
Nil Desperandum (Apex Publishing, 2006)

BLAGGERS INC.
BRITAIN'S BIGGEST ARMED ROBBERIES

TERRY SMITH

Text copyright © 2008 by Terry Smith

The moral right of the author has been asserted.

British Library Cataloguing-in-Publication Data:
A catalogue record for this book is available from
The British Library

ISBN 978-1-906015-19-0

Pennant Books' True Crime series is edited by Paul Woods.

The editor wishes to express his gratitude to Paul Buck,
for his assistance in the completion of this book.

Design & Typeset by Envy Design Ltd

Printed and bound by Grafica Veneta S.p.A., Trebaseleghe (PD) - Italy

Pictures reproduced with kind permission of PA Photos and Getty Images.

Every reasonable effort has been made to acknowledge the ownership of copyright material included in this book. Any errors that have inadvertently occurred will be corrected in subsequent editions provided notification is sent to the publisher.

Pennant Books
A division of Pennant Publishing Ltd
PO Box 5675
London W1A 3FB

www.pennantbooks.com

To Tracey
"The sweetest sweet in existence."
xxx

CONTENTS

ACKNOWLEDGEMENTS

I would like to thank my immediate and extended family, for filling my life with so much joy in their own special ways: Tracey and Sonny; Tel Boy and Marissa; Bradley and Nikki; Jade, Shariff and Abdullah; Iris and Pat; Suzy and Linda; Patsy and Boozie; Jonathan, Jessica and Maisy; Iris, Paul, Alec, Thomas and Olivia; Johnny, Val and family; Fred, Marie and family; Jimmy, Betty and family; Frank, Joyce and family; Leonard Senior, Lenny, LJ, Audrey, Ray, Billy and Carly; Tony, Janice and family; Derek and family.

I would also like to thank the following people (in no particular order) who, in their own various ways, have played a significant role in my development as a true crime writer and consultant:

My publisher and friend Cass Pennant; David Glover; Rudolph Herzog; Oliver, Liza and especially Yvonne Bainton at Windfall Films, who proved invaluable; Geoff

Deehan; Paul Buck; Paul Woods; Chris at Apex; Jim Dawkins; Jack Upson.

Also thanks to Mark, Annette, Cassius Blake and family, and all the fabulous people in Cambridge; Dean, Christine and family and friends in Wisbech; Peter Welch and family; Tony and Mandy; Martin and Kim Bowers, and their families; George and Maggie; Kane and Jo; Robert and Lisa; Tony, Kim and family; Jimmy and Donna; Frank and Queenie; Gary and Sharon Topsfield, and family; Andy and Doreen Rowlands; Harry, Oliver, Lee and the crew at Shores of London; John, Gina, Sonny, Jay and Remi Laveve; Brian Richardson and family; Howard and Toni Prosser; Ivy and family; Tony and Peter Colson; Patsy and Mabel Feeley; Roy Shaw; Joey Pyle; Richard @ Lanmere; Peter and Sue Mitchell; Danny, Tina and family; Nelson and Amber; Dave and Mikki; Steve and Debbie; Steve and Lesley; Ian and Jo; Michael Cole; George and family; Michael and Joe; Karen, Dave and family.

To those in the Big House: Charlie Bronson; Billy Todd; Nozzer; Angelo; Razor Smith; Chris Pearman; Rooky; Mr Kim; Danny Clark; Porky Hunt; Paul Marsh; Del White, and all the lads at Belmarsh.

Special thanks to: Aziz Rahman; Jonathan Lennon; Leonard Smith QC; Darryl Lockwood.

And finally, I would like to thank God the Almighty. Whoever you are, wherever you are, I sense that you are with me.

INTRODUCTION

In the summer of 2007 I received an email from the newest and most exciting publisher on the block, Cass Pennant, who invited me to join his growing team of writers and become a part of the Pennant Crime series. At the time I was already working on several true crime projects involving my specialist subject, armed robbery and those who have participated in it.

Then, in January 2008, Cass called me to say he wanted me to write a book about the world's best blags, a kind of warts-and-all account and analysis of the world's greatest and worst armed robberies. I pointed out that Britain itself possesses a fascinating history of such dramatic crimes committed over the last fifty years.

I also stressed that, unlike orthodox journalists who suck up to the authorities for their primary source material, I would be drawing upon my firsthand knowledge and experience of crime, the British judicial system, long-term imprisonment and life as a fugitive. This would not only qualify me to write about Britain's boldest blags, but also enable me to assess and evaluate both the ingenuity and the flaws inherent in these crimes. More significantly on a personal level, I have often had the privilege to meet and socialise with some of those associated with these legendary armed robberies.

I would like to state from the very outset that the aim of this book is neither to praise nor criticise those who committed the crimes, but to look closely at what went right or wrong when the heists were planned and executed. For critics or cynics wont to accuse this book of promoting criminal methods and techniques, it should also be stressed that all the primary research material used herein has been, at sometime or other, in the public domain. I have, however, digested all the facts in order to give my own personal perspective.

As a modern 'robbologist' – someone who studies the science and methodology of robbery – I know that robbery has been with us since the dawn of time. One can imagine the first serious offence of robbery occurring when a caveman clumped his fellow troglodyte over the head with a cudgel to steal his supper. Then, as man developed and evolved over the centuries, the notion of physically stealing personal property, dwellings, land and even entire countries became *de rigueur* amongst the belligerent colonialists of yesteryear. Hence one man's seemingly legal expropriation of land and property is another's brutal, barefaced robbery.

A more contemporary definition of robbery and robbers

can be found in the excellent book *Armed Robbery* by Roger Matthews, professor of criminology. In the text he states that armed robbers fall into three broad categories: amateur, intermediate and professional.

Understandably, amateur robbers form the largest group as they adopt a spontaneously haphazard, opportunistic approach to crime and are often motivated by desperation. Amateurs frequently act alone and exhibit little or any organisational skill. A typical amateur robber carries out the crime under the influence of drink or drugs in order to settle debts. Such novices generally leave a string of attempted or failed robberies in their wake, committed with poor disguises and imitation firearms, gravitating toward vulnerable targets. Upon capture, a deep sense of embarrassment at their incompetence and the small amount of money taken is a predominant response.

On the other hand, the intermediate robbers also form a substantive group. Having been taught 'the game' by more experienced robbers or by dint of a series of short prison sentences, they are generally more organised. Frequently engaging in a reasonable level of planning, they also tend to work in small groups of three to five individuals, and are more prepared to carry or use a real firearm. Under close examination, however, this disparate group can be subdivided into two further categories, the 'criminal diversifiers' and 'criminal developers'.

Ostensibly, the diversifiers are sporadic blaggers with a

long history of criminal involvement who dabble in a number of more general crimes, such as burglary, car theft, ram-raiding and drug dealing. Invariably, this type of semi-professional robber only becomes active when provided with information about a specific target or invited to participate in a crime planned by others. In many respects, the diversifier is a 'general purpose criminal' who becomes elusively difficult to identify by the very fact that he is governed by opportunity and circumstance. Conversely, however, this freelance approach is perilous as, once under police surveillance for lesser offences, he can contaminate an otherwise 'sterile' group.

As for the 'intermediate developers', these are robbers in a transitional phase who consider themselves potential professionals. They are not merely going along for the ride, like the diversifiers, but are willing to take on more challenging and lucrative targets. Ultimately motivated by a more driving force, the developers adopt and employ more competent modes of planning, disguise, weaponry and escape. The aspiring developer knows that the only way up the tree of criminal prestige is to emulate the style, skill and professionalism of those who he respects.

The professional robbers represent a small elite group. For them, armed robbery is a dedicated career choice which becomes a way of life. Their long-term commitment to stealing high-valued goods and cash pervades every aspect of their character and demeanour. Highly focused and organised, this group aim for more unusual and lucrative targets, spending weeks, even months, planning heists which often entail the use of elaborate disguises, sophisticated equipment and specialist firepower.

Despite having the capability to exhibit extreme violence, however, contrary to the media portrayal of professional robbers, violence is only ever employed in order to seize and secure the prize or to escape. Invariably, professionals take part in high-profile, high-risk crimes where the amount of money taken becomes a mark of status and respect. The proceeds are then used to sustain and maintain an appropriate lifestyle and to reinvest in both legal and illegal business ventures.

Not surprisingly, the central focus of this book is on the upper echelon of armed blaggers, the aristocrats of crime. It takes more than a *soupcon* of boldness and bravado to become a professional robber. We can see from the cases analysed here how inventiveness, intelligence and intuition all play a major role in the planning and execution of high-value heists, and what attributes and qualities it takes to organise a supreme 'bit of work' that goes down in British criminal folklore.

Similarly, as you progress through the chapters you will also learn that the 'perfect crime' is a myth. Crime invariably leaves a trail of witting or unwitting victims in its wake, and its consequences pervade and pollute every atom of society: from those who represent and uphold the criminal justice system right through to the perpetrators and victims of crime, and their families. There are no winners as we all succumb, in one way or another, to crime's darker purpose of inflicting suffering and, ultimately, a kind of failure.

Terry Smith, October 2008

THE GREAT TRAIN ROBBERY

8 AUGUST 1963

When criminologists and connoisseurs of crime reflect on what was the most spectacularly dramatic heist of the twentieth century, the Great Train Robbery has got to be way up in the rankings. For it possesses all the characteristics of a Bond movie: a plot to steal a fortune from the Queen; a dynamic cast; plenty of action, and the myth of a mysterious 'Mr Big' that has grown over the years.

Since I have been researching this crime, I've found it totally incomprehensible how a gang of professionals could rob a train with such clockwork precision and escape with £2.6 million, only for them to leave a goldmine of incriminating evidence for the police at their safe-house. Like the robbery itself, it simply defies comprehension.

When people speak about 'the Train', they immediately focus upon the most well-known and celebrated characters, such as Ronnie Biggs, Buster Edwards and Charlie Wilson.

But, for this chapter, I want to concentrate on the undisputed mastermind of the robbery: Bruce Reynolds.

Born in inner London on 7 September 1931, Bruce's early childhood was not a happy one. He lost his mother, Dorothy, and his sister during childbirth; in the same year, he also lost his grandfather. But this unfathomable sense of loss brought Bruce closer to his endearing grandmother and his father, Thomas. One often hears that, when a child loses a parent at such an early age, the deceased parent supposedly becomes their guardian angel. Whether this is true or not, by the time that the young Reynolds turned to thieving it was clear that he possessed the Midas touch.

But when his father remarried, problems began. Bruce's grandmother noticed that he felt unloved and unwanted, and took him under her wing. The frosty atmosphere in the Reynolds household came to a head one day, when Bruce came home from school to find his beloved pet dog had been put down by his stepmother, Amy, who was expecting a baby. Some say this was the moment that changed the boy, who decided then that he had to seize what he wanted from life. But the more likely explanation is that, like many children, Bruce became addicted to adventure and danger.

At school he used his natural intelligence and perceptiveness to wheel and deal in the playground. He also learned that, to a great extent, diplomacy was a more effective tool than brute force. He put this to good use when he convinced his grandmother to buy him a

Diana .117 air pistol, later taken away by his father when neighbours complained that someone was shooting at their windows.

The teenager's inevitable baptism of fire occurred when he gave a policeman some backchat while out on his pushbike. The policeman jumped into his car and rammed him off the bike, bashing him and driving him to the local nick. This was a complete shock to Bruce, who had never believed that the police wantonly assaulted people. The next day he appeared in court and was fined one pound. Bruce was utterly dumbfounded, and the experience reinforced his burgeoning disdain for those in authority.

In spite of advice from his father, the young Reynolds was determined to follow his instincts and embark upon a life of crime. In between spells of employment as a trainee reporter at Fleet Street and a mechanic at Paris Cycles in Stoke Newington, he was robbing telephone boxes and committing smash-and-grabs. He was first nicked when his accomplice, Cobby, told the police about a smash-and-grab where four air pistols were taken. Bruce was sentenced to borstal training, allocated to Gaynes Hall Borstal in Cambridgeshire. It was reserved for offenders of high intelligence, who were possibly salvageable through education. Reynolds exhibited his intelligence in the only way that he knew, and escaped.

Throughout adolescence and early adulthood, Bruce was in and out of borstal and prison like a proverbial lag. He had been introduced to the austere regimes of

Wormwood Scrubs and Wandsworth, and was gaining an appreciable reputation among the criminal fraternity as a strong, single-minded individual who did not want to be moulded by the prison authorities.

By the time he was released from Reading gaol, aged twenty-one, he wanted to make up for lost time. Instead, he received his call-up papers for National Service. In Bruce's view there was not much difference between prison and army life, so he took off. It wasn't long before he was arrested for breaking and entering, and was sentenced to three years imprisonment with the big boys in adult prison. If borstal was deemed the college of crime, then prison was undeniably its university. Here, in the halls of knowledge and learning, he first recognised that there was no value or profit in just getting nicked and returning to jail. It was time to become professional in his criminal adventures.

After a spell of hoisting (shoplifting) and creeping (entering houses in the dead of night, stealing wallets and jewellery), Bruce entered the twilight world of the 'ladder gangs', made famous by the legendary Peter Scott and George 'Taters' Chatham. Basically, these professional burglars relied upon information from hotel staff, chauffeurs, cleaners and high society magazines which revealed where and when the rich and famous resided during their tenure in Britain.

Once a target and venue were established, the ladder gangs would wait until their targets were sitting down to dinner or sleeping, and enter via a first-floor window to gain their prize. I had the privilege of working on a TV programme with Peter Scott, nicknamed 'the Human Fly', some years ago, and he recounted stories to me about how he would plunder hotels, houses and furriers in the West End. In his day he was, without a doubt, one of the best thieves and money-getters that ever walked the streets of London.

This clandestine world of stealing safes, jewellery and furs by night brought Reynolds into contact with well-known fences. He began to frequent the Star of Belgravia and Marlborough pubs in Chelsea. These watering holes were to become a magnet for artists, actors, gangsters, villains, and even senior detectives with their antennae switched on. Rather than make enemies of the latter, Bruce would occasionally swap drinks and small talk with them.

It's difficult to ascertain what he wanted from his criminal career at this time. Did he want to be low-profile, the man behind the scenes, earning a small fortune and remaining unnoticed? Or did he want to become the super-villain with contacts in every dark corner of criminal life, including the law?

History illustrates how the unholy coalescence of criminals and crooked cozzers is a recipe for disaster. The crook believes that he is being ultra-clever by having such a well-connected contact, but the copper knows that the profit from the liaison will only flow one way. The crook is on borrowed time.

Evidence of this came when there was a fatality on a 'bit of work' in Colliers Wood, south London. The police called at Bruce's grandmother's place in Battersea and left a note telling him to contact Wandsworth police station. Bruce visited the station, gave a statement outlining his whereabouts on the specific day, and was left in no doubt by the friendly chief inspector on the other side of the counter that his activities, the places he habituated, his friends and acquaintances were all well known to the Old Bill.

The corollary remains: high-profile equates with high-danger; low-profile corresponds with safety and survival.

Bruce was going from strength to strength, progressing from the relatively innocuous ladder gangs to gelignite raids. Based upon sound information, he and his gang travelled the length and breadth of Britain to blow safes, plundering the banknotes and jewellery within. His natural drive and ambition were complemented by his personal style and taste. After each successful criminal caper, Reynolds would hop into his Aston Martin and drive to the French Riviera, visiting the best restaurants and beaches along the Cote d'Azur. For he learned at a very early stage in his career that there was no point waiting for Old Bill to knock on your door, when you could be eating lobster and sipping Dom Pérignon in Cannes. He was soon well versed in the acquired art of pleasurable decadence.

As the name 'Bruce Reynolds' became synonymous with success, offers and information were coming in from every angle. Admittedly he had the occasional setback, like three and a half years imprisonment for a botched attempt to rob a bookmaker. But it was inevitable that he would push the boundaries even further, and venture into the aristocratic ranks of the armed robber.

What we have to remember is that, in the early 1960s, the security industry was in its infancy. There were no laminated screens, airlock entry systems or data tracking of security vehicles. It was the caveman era, when the chained strongbox and pickaxe handle reigned supreme.

Bruce and his partner, Harry, decided it was time to join forces with Buster Edwards, Charlie Wilson and Gordon Goody to attack a Securicor van delivering wages to a railway depot at Old Oak Common, northwest London. On the day of the robbery they backed their van into the doors of the wages office, escaping with £30,000. This was considered a small fortune at the time.

Once Reynolds and his new gang members got the taste for well-organised armed raids, there was no looking back. The next bit of work was based upon information from a security guard. A security van used the same route every Wednesday night to return to headquarters. Due to staff shortages the three-man team was currently reduced to two, the guards sitting in the front of the van, leaving access to the rear unhindered. In true bravura fashion, Reynolds decided to ram the security van head-on, while other members of the gang boxed it in from behind.

Once it was clear the security van was going nowhere,

the guards jumped out and Wilson started unloading boxes of cash. These were then loaded into the getaway car, before they roared away to their changeover vehicle with takings of £60,000. The whole exercise was over in three minutes. Confidence was sky-high among the gang. They noted that, with a dynamic combination of boldness, split-second timing and the element of surprise, anything was possible.

It was during this *belle époque* of armed robberies that Reynolds received information about the Post Office transporting cash and valuables via rail. This was not news to the robbers, but, unlike established private and commercial security companies that practically broadcast how they were carrying large amounts of cash, the Post Office espoused a low-security approach using unmarked vehicles and mailbags. The only way to find out about the contents of these nondescript vehicles was from inside information.

Over the years, Bruce had been drawing steadily closer to his lifelong quest for the Big One. His interest was initially piqued when a railway worker told him about a bank manager friend of his, who let him into a bank at Redhill to see £1 million in cash. The bank manager added that they used the Royal Mail regularly to transport huge sums of money. Bruce slipped down to Redhill Station with Jimmy White, to look at the work. Sure enough, there were mailbags piled high on the platform. But deciding which contained the mail and which the cash was impossible without inside information, so they decided to shelve the plan.

The next project looked more promising. Bruce received information from his man in the Midlands about a Royal Mail lorry delivering money to Redditch station. This was the football pools money en route to King's Cross station, in London. Along with other cash amounts collected from stations on the way, it was transported under heavy security to William Hill's head office at the Barbican. Recognising that the information held some credence, Bruce and Harry snatched the money being delivered to Redditch and escaped with £3000. In conjunction with the rest of the gang, their original plan had been to rob the entire pools consignment as it arrived at the Barbican. It was scuppered, however, when their inside man told them that some betting offices sent cheques instead of cash.

Then, in late 1962, Bruce was told that heavy metal boxes containing railway workers' wages were loaded onto the Irish Mail train at Paddington station, destined for Swindon. Buster and Goody found the information to be sound, but the security during the loading of the wages at Paddington was tight. And so a plan was hatched whereby the communication cord of the train would be pulled between stations on the outskirts of London, and the robbers would break into the guard's coach at the rear to seize their prize.

A test run worked perfectly. As planned, the communication cord was pulled and the train stopped by a disused factory at West Drayton. On the day of the robbery itself, Bruce, Buster, Goody and Wilson waited until the train had passed Ealing. Then, armed with crowbars and bolt croppers, they made their way to the guard's coach. Goody smashed open the door and confronted the solitary guard.

The rest of the gang attacked the cashboxes that were chained to the carriage floor. The communication cord had been pulled but the train refused to stop. Reynolds noticed that they were going past their pickup point at the disused factory. Edwards had the presence of mind, however, to apply the brakes manually by turning a huge steering wheel.

By the time the train stopped, the gang were a mile away from the pickup point. They jumped onto the track and ran with the heavy metal cashboxes. Puffing and panting, they finally reached their getaway van, but only the super-fit Goody still held a cashbox. When they finally got back to base, they found it contained £700. It was a rude awakening, a good bit of work ruined by poor planning.

The Airport Robbery

Desperate to make amends for the Irish Mail train fiasco, Charlie Wilson came up with some information regarding wages for the entire BOAC staff at London Airport. Every Tuesday morning, a security van would pull up at Barclay's Bank on the south perimeter of the airport. It would wheel out a strongbox on a trolley containing a rumoured £300,000 to £400,000 for the workers. This would be loaded into the security van for the journey to Comet House, a four-storey office building some hundred yards away. Normally the security van was accompanied by three civilian cashiers, and occasionally a police escort.

Buster Edwards and Gordon Goody, dressed in executive attire, travelled down to the airport to produce a viable plan. While Goody waited in the foyer of the building, Edwards visited a toilet on the third floor. From the toilet window he could see not only the bank, but also the roof of the security van as it pulled up at Comet House. Logic dictated that, if the gang were in the toilet when the security van pulled up, they could take the elevator down and intercept the security guards with the strongbox. Once the prize was seized, the gang would take off in stolen vehicles along a perimeter side-road, through a wire-mesh gate to the changeover vehicle.

The night before the proposed raid, a padlock was cut on the perimeter wire. On the day of the robbery, posing as executive job hunters in bowler hats and pinstripe suits, with iron bars concealed inside their umbrellas, Bruce, Charlie, Buster, Gordon and Billy Jennings made their way up to the third-floor toilet. Harry remained in the foyer while Roy James and Mickey Ball were at the steering wheels of two powerful Jaguars. Everything was set to go, when they noticed the security van had a police escort and the robbery was aborted.

The gang rescheduled the raid for the following week,

but they noticed someone had replaced the lock on the wire-mesh gate. They decided to replace the chain with a false link that cleverly came apart. This time, the robbery came off as planned.

On Tuesday 20 November 1962, the security van pulled up outside Comet House; the guards unloaded the trolley and wheeled it into the foyer. Once the elevator had descended to the ground floor, out came five heavily-disguised men with coshes held aloft. After a few deft blows to the guards and attendant cashiers, the robbers loaded the trolley's contents into the Jags and powered away down the perimeter side road.

During the *melee*, however, Goody had dropped his checked cap in the foyer. As they could not find the false link on the fence, bolt croppers had been used to cut the chain, and these were left in a stolen Jaguar. Back at the count-out, they opened the strongbox and discovered £62,500 in wages. After paying expenses, the eight robbers had netted £6,000 each for their troubles.

The raid attracted significant media attention. The Metropolitan Police's infamous Flying Squad were put on the case, and started rounding up potential suspects.

A day after the raid, Wilson, Goody and the drivers, James and Ball, were swagged in by the squad. Over the next several weeks a series of identification parades were held at Cannon Row and Twickenham police stations. Charlie and Gordon were picked out by witnesses at the scene of the robbery, while Ball was mistakenly identified as Billy

Jennings, who bought the bolt croppers from an ironmonger. Evidently, the ironmonger thought Jennings looked suspicious, following him out of the shop and watching him get into Goody's Jaguar. As was his custom, Reynolds was long gone; Paris, Tangiers and Gibraltar beckoned.

In the months preceding the trial, Goody managed to channel some money through his well-connected solicitor, Brian Field, and apply for bail which was conveniently unopposed by the police. For £1500, Field also managed to get Reynolds' name removed from the list of suspects.

During the trial Mickey Ball got cold feet, decided to make a deal and pleaded guilty to being a driver on the raid. He copped five years imprisonment. Charlie Wilson was acquitted by the judge after a defence submission that the identification evidence was unsafe. And Gordon Goody was left with a witness from the foyer claiming he was the robber wearing a checked cap; another witness on a double-decker bus said he saw Goody get out of the stolen Jaguar in the Comet House car park, while the ironmonger had taken down the registration number of the car driven by the man who bought the bolt croppers, now forensically linked to the chain on the fence.

In isolation the evidence could be diluted, even discredited, but taken altogether its cumulative effect suggested guilt. Goody had to act fast. The only option he had was to try to slip into the jury. He and Buster Edwards tracked an amiable looking jury member to Finchley Road, north London, where they offered him cash for the right verdict. The man refused the cash, as he had served some time in prison himself. The next day, the jury were sent out. After hours of deliberation they were unable to return a verdict. A retrial was ordered.

Before the retrial, Goody decided to bolster his defence by getting his solicitor to hire a bus and an independent photographer to take photos of the Comet House car park. It was proven that the witness on the bus could not have seen him getting out of the stolen Jaguar. For £200, Gordon also got a bent cozzer to replace the cap with one three sizes bigger, so that when he was asked to try it on in the witness box it came down over his face and ears. The ironmonger was still adamant that it was Mickey Ball he saw getting into Gordon's Jaguar. But, at the retrial, Goody got the person who actually bought the bolt croppers to sit in the courtroom, so now the witness was not so sure after all.

After a persuasive display by the defence counsel, Goody was acquitted. As always, the case had not been about discerning the truth but about who could put forward the most convincing argument. As Goody left the courtroom, he walked up to the prosecution bench and picked up the chain with the false link and exclaimed, "Your forensic expert cannot be that good as they did not notice this, eh?" He then revealed how the false link came apart. The prosecutor was agog, Gordon was cock-a-hoop, but the Flying Squad were seething and wanted revenge. They would not make the same mistake twice.

Once the dust had settled over the airport robbery, Reynolds and his team were itching to strike again. Information was still trickling in from reliable sources, but there was nothing to get the adrenalin pumping. A former photographer, turned British Rail porter at Waterloo, mentioned shipments of gold that came from South Africa to Southampton on a regular basis. They were then transported by rail to Waterloo, where they were greeted by Bank of England officials and the police. The gang embarked upon lengthy observations at both Southampton docks and Waterloo station, but the logistics of stopping a train and stealing a ton of gold were nightmarish.

Then there was mention of a money train that collected cash at almost every station from Bournemouth on the South Coast to London. The train's last stop before Waterloo was Weybridge in Surrey. That following Tuesday, Bruce Reynolds and his partner, John Daly, were plotted up in the undergrowth on the embankment at 3am, when two police cars screeched up on either side of Weybridge station. Initially, Reynolds and Daly thought that they had been spotted, or had walked into a trap. But when they saw the cozzers alight from their vehicles and engage in light banter, they knew that they were present to safeguard the money.

Not long afterwards, Bruce heard the familiar sound of a Royal Mail truck. It reversed up to the entrance of the station and awaited its load. The train was on time, transferring seven large bags of cash into the truck, which was then driven to the main post office at Weybridge High Street. The inside information was correct, save for one point: the train was not collecting money, it was delivering it.

Back at base, Reynolds conveyed these observations to the rest of the gang, who pitched in with their own points: How much money was in the mailbags? What about the police, how would they deal with them?

Moreover, someone had broken into Jimmy White's lock-up garages and stolen their getaway vehicles and other equipment. In short, the plan to rob the Weybridge train had lost its momentum and impetus. Most professional villains work on their instincts, and if something is not right then it's better to call it off. As the old adage says, the police only have to be lucky once whereas the professional villain has to be lucky all the time.

The Train Robbery

Just as Bruce, Buster and the gang were licking their wounds over the Bournemouth money train saga, Brian Field, their solicitor, came up with another interesting proposition. Brian had represented Edwards and Goody in many criminal law proceedings, and over the years a significant rapport had developed between them. Not only was he an excellent mouthpiece, he had become a reliable source of information – including sound advice about where cash and valuables were kept in country houses.

In early 1963, Field claimed he had first-class inside information about a regular Glasgow to London train carrying mailbags full of cash. He had liaised with the inside man he called 'the Ulsterman' on a bench in Finsbury Park. At the meet, the Ulsterman provided a cornucopia of valuable information about the train. He said it travelled throughout the night, stopping at stations along the way to collect cash consignments. He added that the money was stored in a High Value Coach (HVC), which was always the second along from the diesel locomotive.

Most significantly, he said that the train – otherwise referred to as a Travelling Post Office (TPO) – transported between fifty to eighty bags of cash, sometimes even more over the bank holiday period. There were five postal workers inside the HVC and another seventy sorters in a coach further along the train.

Upon hearing the information about the night train, Reynolds immediately recognised its potential. In his view, there was nothing like spot-on inside information. His mind was racing at the prospect of organising such a raid, only this time he did not want it to end up like the Irish Mail train saga. With the successful London Airport robbery still fresh in their minds, the only thing that concerned the gang was the possibility of a police sting, whereby the gang's audacity and greed could lure them (even chaperone them) into a well-crafted trap. Bruce tossed these negative thoughts aside, coming to the conclusion that there was no value in wallowing in paranoia. His instincts felt good; he knew that this was going to be the mother of all robberies.

Several covert meetings were called among the gang, with a series of compelling questions put forward: Where were they going to stop the train? How were they going to stop the train? How would they gain access to the High Value Coach? And how would they reach the safety of home?

This was where the mastermind Bruce Reynolds came into his own. He was a superb organiser of logistics and resources. He had been planning successful raids on country houses, factories, safes, banks and security vans all his adult life, and this job was to be his baby. He could feel it in his water that this was going to be the Big One.

Out of mutual respect and deference to Bruce's criminal achievements, the rest of the gang allowed him to put his plans in motion. Buster and Charlie would watch the Glasgow to London train arrive at Euston, and confirm that money was indeed unloaded. Bruce and Gordon would look for a possible strike point along the Glasgow to London line.

After surveying Ordnance Survey maps and travelling along the relevant train line, Reynolds sensed there was no way that the train could be stopped in a built-up, urban area. He knew it had to happen in the relatively serene surroundings of the countryside. This brought added problems, however, as experience taught that getting home from such remote locations after committing a crime was very difficult. Prisons were full of luckless criminals caught in the no man's land between town and country. Bruce knew that one option was to find a flop or safe-house, a reasonable distance away from the crime, where the robbers could sit safe until the heat had evaporated.

After a considerable amount of observation and research, he located the perfect spot to stop the train. The place he chose was Sears Crossing, between Leighton Buzzard and Cheddington stations in Buckinghamshire. What appealed to him was that the B488 road ran parallel to the track and cut underneath the line at Bridego Bridge. Reynolds came up with a plan to stop the train somewhere in between these two stations and drive it to the remote bridge, where they could attack the High Value Coach, transfer the money into a lorry and escape. During his reconnaissance of the area, he noted that there was an army base at Bicester and came up with the idea of the robbers impersonating an expedition force out on night-time manoeuvres. This would fit in with the country surroundings and dispel any doubts and suspicions amongst the local farming community.

Back at base another meet was called, where Bruce, Buster, Gordon, Charlie, Jimmy, Roy and John Daly trawled through all the ideas that had arisen from their research. The main problem was how the gang were going to stop a hundred-ton train travelling at over eighty mph without alerting all the postal workers inside the coaches.

The answer was to stop it by tampering with the railway's traffic-light signal system. Buster mentioned that another gang on the South Coast, who he knew well, had been successfully stopping trains in their area and robbing them. In fact, there had been similar raids at Kingston and Brighton. The only remedy, therefore, was to invite the other gang along. They agreed that there was enough money to go around, and that the extra manpower would be beneficial. Further, the South Coast robbers were said to go very discreetly about their business.

At the next meeting, Buster brought along Roger Cordrey, a signals specialist, Tommy Wisbey, an ex-army boxer, Jimmy Hussey and Bob Welch. They all went through the plans, democratically voting on important issues such as how and where to stop the train, and the best mode of escape. They all agreed (save for Roy James) that the best idea was to find a safe-house about twenty to thirty miles away from Bridego Bridge, where they could all lay up and count out the money, dispersing after the heat had died down. James favoured the notion of putting as much distance between the crime and themselves as possible, even suggesting that they motored all the way back to the relative anonymity of London. Alas, he was outvoted on this, and Reynolds set about finding a suitable safe-house in the Buckinghamshire area.

After ascertaining the general direction of escape from the train line, he traced a secluded farm for sale about thirty miles by road from the bridge. Totally uncharacteristically and with a degree of arrogance, Reynolds knocked on the door to be shown around Leatherslade Farm and its two outbuildings by the owner, Mr Rixon, and his wife.

I don't know what Bruce Reynolds was thinking when he put his face up on show to view the property, as this was sheer suicide. Here was a high-profile super-crook, with a well-known reputation for organising and executing big-time robberies, speaking to a potential witness to what could become the crime of the century.

In his mitigation, however, from experience I know how he must have felt. He was the driving force behind the project, and he did not want it to flounder and lose impetus like the Bournemouth money train saga. He was the motivator and the financier who wanted to get things moving. But with the benefit of hindsight, even Reynolds knows that this was a supreme act of folly.

The situation was further exacerbated by Brian Field overseeing the purchase of the farm from the estate agent. Field, who worked for a firm of solicitors owned by an ex-army officer called John Wheater, recruited Lenny Field (no relation) to be the nominal purchaser. It was bought for £5,500 by a traceable and identifiable purchaser and a solicitor acting on his behalf. Should the farm be located after the robbery, there was a definite paper trail leading to Brian Field and, by association, his erstwhile criminal clients Edwards, Goody, and all those suspected of the London Airport robbery.

The location of the farm was pivotal to the success of the whole operation. If it were found, a domino effect of arrest and incarceration would ensue. Naturally, Reynolds was banking on the fact that it would *not* be.

By now he had polished and refined the plan to stop the train. He liked the notion of using bogus army vehicles to get to and from the scene of the robbery, buying a Bedford truck and a Land Rover from a car auction, and stealing another Land Rover from central London. All these vehicles were repainted in the traditional army livery of khaki and yellow. He also obtained handcuffs, walkie-talkies, combat uniforms, camping equipment, a VHF radio receiver and ample food and provisions to feed all the gang at the farm.

In the gospel according to Bruce Reynolds, one of the central precepts of any crime was to always keep things simple. Complicated plans only led to confusion and turmoil. The art of success was literally simplicity itself. Therefore Reynolds broke the plan into three easy stages:

Stage one. Bruce would position himself eight hundred yards south of Leighton Buzzard train station. He would contact the whole gang via walkie-talkies to alert them that the train was approaching. Simultaneously, the dwarf signal would be altered to amber in order to slow the train down and the red light on the gantry changed so that the train would stop at Sears Crossing.

Stage two. Once the train had responded to the red light and stopped, railway procedure dictated that the driver would alight from the locomotive to contact the signalman via a trackside telephone. The first assault team would then overpower the train driver and fireman, uncouple the carriages carrying the postal sorters and force the train driver to drive the locomotive to Bridego Bridge, for the final assault.

Stage three. The combined assault team would then attack the High Value Coach from different sections and force entry into the carriage. They would handcuff the postal workers and pass the money down the embankment, via a human chain, into the bogus army lorry. Once all the robbers were on board and accounted for, the lorry would set off in convoy through the countryside to the safe-house.

After he explained the plan there was a debate about whether the train would stop. Quite simply, Reynolds answered, if the train did not stop then they would drive away and come back another day. There was also unease about whether or not the locomotive driver would comply with their demands. Unanimously, the gang decided that the best idea was to find their own driver, rather than placing their hopes in the hands of a solitary British Rail employee.

This problem was solved almost by accident. When Reynolds went on a weekend social visit to see his old friend Ronnie Biggs in Redhill, Surrey, Biggs mentioned that he was painting the bungalow of an old boy who used to be a train driver. Startled by the coincidence, Bruce asked if the old boy would be up for a bit of action. Without revealing too much detail, he outlined the plan.

Biggs approached Peter, the train driver, who was offered £40,000 for his services. Peter agreed to the deal, although he confessed he had no experience of driving the big English Electric diesel locomotives. But basically, he said, the controls were all the same.

The only problem for Reynolds was that Ronnie Biggs wanted to be part of the robbery. At the next meeting it was put to the rest of the gang, and both Ronnie and the engine driver were accepted onto the team.

When Reynolds was satisfied that everything was ready for action, a message was sent to the Ulsterman to set a date for the raid. There was some concern that the Glasgow to London night flyer had begun to use a secure, modern High Value Coach as opposed to the older, more run-down version. The Ulsterman reassured the robbers that, on the night of the raid, the older version would be in the rolling stock.

This made Reynolds wonder what position the inside man held in the railway industry. Was he a porter, a postal worker, an engineer, or even a mysterious Mr Big on the management side? The Ulsterman was also aware that there would be extra cash on the train over the bank holiday weekend. Was he therefore a bank official? A security advisor? An office clerk? Whatever the case, the message came through that the robbery was set for the early hours of the morning of Wednesday 7 August 1963.

The day before the robbery, all of the gang gathered at Leatherslade Farm near Oakley, Buckinghamshire – except Gordon Goody, who was to take the all-important telephone call from the Ulsterman at a remote countryside payphone. As the warm August day turned to dusk, nervous tension and anticipation began to rise in the gang. Some relied on light banter and humour to dispel the unease, while others were already counting their share of the money and mentally sunbathing on a yacht in the Mediterranean.

Later than expected, Gordon arrived with the news that the robbery was not to go ahead that evening. They would all have to go through the same process the following day. To the more experienced members of the gang, this was nothing unusual. Frequently, major bits of work were postponed for the purposes of survival or extra cash, or just due to an unforeseen delay.

Patience may not seem like the most natural state of mind prior to a spectacular robbery. But when you can double or even triple the prize, a smidgeon of composure and self-restraint is well worth it. To while away the time, some of the gang played Monopoly, some drank beer and some cooked meals. As for Peter, the train driver, he was enjoying the warm atmosphere of camaraderie; he had not been among such fine company for years.

The next day, there was a knock on the farm door and everybody froze. No one wanted to answer it for fear of being recognised at a later date. Reynolds opened the door. It was a neighbouring farmer, Mr Wyatt, who wanted to continue his pre-existing arrangement for the rental of the adjoining fields. Coolly, Bruce explained that he was only the decorator, but he would pass the request on to the owner when he next saw him.

Once again, he had put his face up on show and knew
that it could prove costly. But he was so far in that it
would have been embarrassing or detrimental to his
criminal career to turn back. The Holy Grail was now
within his grasp, and nothing short of an act of God was
going to prevent him from fulfilling his destiny.

Later that evening, they all received the news that they
had been waiting for: the show was on. The gang put on
their army fatigues and climbed into the back of the
Bedford army truck. Reynolds slipped on his blue beret,
with the wings of the Special Air Services' insignia
attached, and led the convoy in his Land Rover. This was
the part he enjoyed the most – after many weeks of
planning and preparation, the domino effect of the crime
would soon go into momentum.

The train had already left Glasgow by the time the
convoy was making its way to Bridego Bridge. Jack Mills,
the train driver, and David Whitby, the fireman, had to
stop at Crewe, Tamworth and Rugby before punching
south to Buckinghamshire. The thirty-minute journey to
the bridge was uneventful, apart from the presence of a
solitary hitchhiker beside a main road.

The convoy arrived at the bridge at 1:30am, the gang
gathering around Bruce to go over the plan one last time.
From the initial trainspotter to the gantry men and the
assault team, everyone knew their role. They were all in
position by 2:45am, at which time the walkie-talkies
were tested.

Then, in the warm cloudless night, Reynolds could see the sidelights of the train coming towards him. Almost imperceptibly at first, the rail began to tingle under his feet, and then the thunder of the powerful diesel engine became ominous. He sent the message for the dwarf and gantry signals to be activated. Already the train driver was applying the brakes, as the great beast was gradually brought to a halt at Sears Crossing. Bruce hopped into the Land Rover and drove down the road parallel to the track. He picked up John Daly, who had operated the dwarf signal, and, as he drove passed the stationary train, he could see Roy James and Jimmy White uncoupling the coaches.

By now the first assault team had overpowered Whitby, the fireman, who had left the train to contact the signal box by telephone. Peter, their own driver, was quickly ushered into the cabin and told to drive the train the short distance to Bridego Bridge. But he was unable to "get a vacuum" in order to move it along. Panic briefly ensued, until someone shouted "get the other driver in here!" Compelled to cooperate by a blow to the head, Mills was forced to drive the train to a marker placed at the bridge.

(Popular legend has it that Mills was coshed rather than punched. But the police talked up their story to negate any public sympathy for the robbers. Buster Edwards later took the blame for the 'coshing' in Piers Paul Read's book, *The Train Robbers*, but anyone who knows about the case also knows that the robber who punched the driver remains unknown and uncaught to this day.)

As the train stopped at the marker, Edwards, Wilson, Goody, Wisbey, Bob Welch and Jimmy Hussey set about the High Value Coach with sledgehammers and crowbars. The entry was swift; the four postal workers inside were quickly pushed to one end of the coach and handcuffed, while another member of the gang bolt-cropped the padlock on the cage holding the cash. Within minutes, the gang had formed a human chain down the embankment and the mailbags, replete with used banknotes, were being passed into the army truck. After removing a hundred and twenty mailbags, Reynolds called time. The gang left eight mailbags behind, one on the embankment.

Quickly and efficiently, the gang piled into their army truck and Land Rovers, disappearing into the country lanes. By the time the convoy had reached Leatherslade Farm, the dawn chorus was in full song. As far as they were concerned, no one had seen them leave or return to the farm.

But the owl-like Miss Nappin, resident at a nearby farm, did not miss a thing. She saw the army truck drive past her property in the early hours and heard it return. Nothing got pass the sleepless spinster.

At Leatherslade Farm the gang stacked the mailbags in the hallway and front room. The robbers began to rip the bags open and tip the contents on the floor. Gordon Goody checked every one for homing devices. It took them three hours to stack the money, ready for counting. As the early morning rays of sunlight beamed through the windows, the VHF receiver was abuzz with activity. One cozzer said, "You ain't gonna believe this, someone has nicked a train!"

By now Reynolds was absolutely exhausted. Like a mad inventor fussing over his patent, he had barely slept over the last twenty-four hours. He took one last look at the mountain of banknotes piled on the floor, and surrendered to sleep. A deep and troubled sleep, although as yet he had little idea of how his name would be etched onto the pantheon of criminal history.

When he woke up, Buster Edwards brought him good tidings; the train robbers had stolen £2,631,000 (equivalent to £40 million in 2008). After £40,000 had been pulled out for Peter the driver and expenses, each member of the gang received £150,000 – including the elusive Ulsterman, who also got his whack. Initially the plan was for the gang to remain at the farm for up to three or four days, but news coverage of the robbery went all the way around the world. An unthinkable amount of untraceable banknotes had been stolen, and the robbery was being trumpeted as 'the Crime of the Century'. Regular news bulletins were being broadcast on TV and radio. But initially the police were in total chaos, and Scotland Yard were inevitably called in to assist the local Buckinghamshire Constabulary.

The first real concern at the hideout came when the robbers heard that an airman had spotted an army truck in the early hours of the morning. Then a police spokesman proclaimed that they were checking all industrial properties and farmhouses within a thirty-mile radius of the robbery. Although Leatherslade Farm was thirty miles away by road, it was only seventeen and a half miles in a straight line. Some of the gang also feared that Mr Wyatt, the neighbouring farmer, may have spotted their army truck when he called about renting the field, two days prior to the robbery.

Tension and restlessness were rising as a meeting was called. The gang decided to clear up the farm and leave the premises as soon as possible. Reynolds has claimed that the gang cleaned every surface and every object at the farm. Some had the presence of mind to wear their gloves all the time; others were not so thorough. The gang started to burn some of the debris from the robbery in the stove, but someone pointed out that smoke would look odd coming from a chimney in the middle of a sweltering summer. It was agreed that, after they had all departed, Goody would pay a close friend a reputed £20,000 to come back to the farm and destroy all the remaining evidence. Henceforth, it was every man for himself.

This was another momentous mistake. Reynolds had been particularly thorough in the planning and execution of the robbery, but they were now making rash *ad hoc* decisions about the disposal of incriminating evidence. In any event, the gang successfully departed with their loot but no one returned to clean the property. But apportioning blame over this substantive error is unjustified, as it is a common feature among some seemingly professional robbers that, once they have pocketed their whack, they believe the crime is over.

Personally, I believe that Bruce Reynolds and some of the others should have returned to the farm once they had stashed their money, and either removed all the evidence, including the vehicles, or burned the entire building down. Admittedly, Reynolds thought it unlikely that the farm would be discovered, but when your life and liberty is at stake, as the old saying goes, it's always better safe than sorry.

During the following days, there was no decrease in media attention. In fact it intensified. In the newspapers, page after page was dedicated to the robbery. The *London Evening Standard* referred to the 'Biggest Ever Mail Robbery'; 'Angry questions were being asked last night about how the world's greatest train robbery could have happened,' opened the *Daily Express* coverage, virtually christening the caper. They also acknowledged that the haul could top £2.5 million. The spectacular crime was a national talking point, even reaching the corridors of power at Westminster. Such was the outcry that insurance companies put up a huge reward of £260,000 for the capture and conviction of the culprits. This was a massive incentive to the vulture-like informants who picked on the victuals of others' crimes.

What concerned the robbers most, however, was that the Metropolitan Police's infamous Flying Squad had been brought in to handle the London end of the enquiry. At the helm of the squad was Chief Superintendent Tommy Butler, a notorious thief-taker who preferred the kudos of a conviction to the self-interest of a bribe. He'd been fast-tracked from detective sergeant to head of the Flying Squad in ten years, but would not baulk at bending the rules a tad to get results. A lifelong bachelor who lived with his mother, the Great Train Robbery enquiry would prove to be the apex of his career.

You can almost feel the immense pressure he was under to get results. The last thing the Conservative government wanted at this time was another embarrassment. The Tory party already had to come to terms with the political scandal of the Profumo affair, after the Secretary of State for War, John Profumo, had been shagging a showgirl mistress, Christine Keeler, who was bestowing the same favours on a known Russian spy, Eugene Ivanov.

Combine this with the embarrassing defection to Russia of a high-ranking member of British intelligence, Kim Philby, and the opposition's call for a general election, and it's little wonder if Butler was given unlimited discretionary authority to arrest, charge and convict the robbers. In his eyes this was the ultimate insult to the Establishment, almost an act of war. Now, with no umpires or rules to ensure fair play, anything was permissible.

The Flying Squad's first breakthrough came five days after the robbery, when the police received a call from a suspicious farm labourer who spotted an army truck at Leatherslade Farm. Bruce Reynolds and Buster Edwards were about to take matters into their own hands and revisit the farm when, on 13 August, the news media reported that the robbers' hideout had been discovered.

At that moment, Reynolds realised it was only a matter of time before Butler and his posse of hard-bitten detectives were onto him. Bruce also knew that, once the Flying Squad got hold of Brian Field, the bent solicitor, he would tell them all that he knew – and what he did not know, he might make up. For once solicitors find themselves on the wrong side of the cell door, the floodgates begin to open.

The second significant breakthrough came when a member of the South Coast raiders, Roger Cordrey, was nicked with £141,000. Cordrey and a friend, Billy Boal – who had nothing to do with the robbery – were arrested when they rented a lock-up garage from a policeman's widow in Bournemouth. She became suspicious when they paid three months' rent in advance in ten-shilling notes. Both were charged with the robbery and remanded in custody.

Meanwhile, back at Leatherslade Farm, Detective Superintendent Maurice Ray, a fingerprint expert at Scotland Yard, was put in charge of sweeping the farm, vehicles and outbuildings for prints. He claimed it was all one big clue, and alluded to arrests being imminent.

At the Yard, due to the significant size of the reward, information from informants was swamping the enquiry room. One prisoner in jail contacted the 'train squad' through his barrister, claiming to know all the names of those that partook in the raid. When this was compared with the list of suspects the Flying Squad already had, it was practically identical.

More contentiously, in order to expedite arrests, the bigshots at the Yard had overruled senior officers in the Flying Squad to authorise the release of photographs of several suspected robbers and their spouses to the national newspapers and TV. This exasperated the enquiry team, as it forewarned Reynolds, Edwards, John Daly and Jimmy White and enabled them to go to ground. Unfortunately, Charlie Wilson was arrested at an address in Clapham the same day as the photographs were released to the news media.

In order to intensify their dragnet, the police were raiding up to fifty addresses a day. Some of the train robbers, like Tommy Wisbey, tried to face police enquiries with readymade alibis, but once their witnesses were confronted with fingerprint evidence from the farm the alibis crumbled. Over the coming weeks the robbers were rounded up like cattle. Roy James was arrested after a rooftop chase in Swiss Cottage. John Daly was collared at a luxury apartment in Belgravia. Brian Field had been a suspect from the very outset, having worked as a clerk for the solicitors who bought Leatherslade Farm and represented clients including Goody. Field was arrested after the discovery of a bag containing £100,000 in

Dorking Woods, with a receipt at the bottom from a boarding house in Germany where he had stayed.

By 10 December, some twelve weeks after the raid, Ronnie Biggs, Jimmy Hussey, Gordon Goody, Bobby Welch, Lenny Field and John Wheater had also been arrested, charged and remanded in custody.

The Trial

The show trial started on 24 January 1964. Aylesbury District Council Chamber had been converted into a makeshift courtroom, in order to cater for the large number of counsel and defendants. The reasons for choosing Aylesbury Assizes (as crown courts were then known) over the Old Bailey, in central London, were that it was near to the scene of the crime, and it was also believed that it would be more difficult to nobble the jury. In the hot seat was His Honour Justice Edmund Davis, with Mr Arthur E. James QC and Mr N. MacDermot QC prosecuting.

At the heart of the prosecution case was forensic evidence linking all the defendants to Leatherslade Farm. It was claimed that, in the relatively relaxed surroundings of the hideout, members of the gang had removed their gloves and literally decorated the property with their finger and palm prints: Charlie Wilson's fingerprints were found on a drum of salt, Ronnie Biggs' on a tomato sauce bottle, with Roy James' prints found on the bottom of a Pyrex plate from when he fed the cats outside the backdoor of the farm – and so on, *ad nauseum*.

The only defendants whose prints were not found at the farm were Gordon Goody and Billy Boal. In Goody's case, it was alleged that the police raided a room that he rented at the Windmill pub in Blackfriars, where they seized a pair of brown suede shoes with specks of yellow and khaki paint identical to yellow paint spilt at the farm, and khaki paint on the pedals of the Land Rover and Bedford truck used in the raid. It appears that the Flying Squad had long memories, with his boast about the false fence link used on the London Airport job returning to haunt Goody. They were not going to let him slip out of this one.

In Boal's case, it was alleged that, when he was arrested in Bournemouth with his friend Cordrey, the police found a brass knob inside the lining of his coat. Traces of yellow paint were found on it that were supposedly identical to that spilt at the robbers' hideout. Outside the courtroom, all the robbers swore that they never knew Boal before the robbery and that he had never been to the farm.

So how did the yellow paint travel from a farm in Buckinghamshire to Billy Boal's pocket in Bournemouth? Was it an act of unlimited discretionary authority on behalf of the investigation squad? Or was it a case of accidental transference? I will leave you to decide. Alas, Billy Boal was found guilty and sentenced to twenty-four years' imprisonment, during which he died, leaving a widow and three children.

After the prosecution's case concluded, Mr Wilfred Fordham QC, defence counsel for John Daly, submitted that there was no case to answer for his client. For although Daly did not deny that his fingerprints were on a Monopoly board found at the farm, he claimed that he had played a game of Monopoly some weeks earlier at an address in south London and that, as a movable object, the board game had been taken to the farm by someone else. It was not proof that Daly was at the farm and, seeing as there was no rebuttal evidence to the contrary, there was no case to answer. The judge agreed, and ordered the jury to acquit.

As expected, the remaining fingerprint evidence and comparison of paint particles proved crucial. The jury agreed that the defendants were all at the farm and had taken part in the robbery. Prior to sentencing, Justice Davis announced:

"[This is] . . . a crime which in its impudence and enormity is the first of its kind in this country. I propose to do all in my power to ensure that it is the last of its kind; for your outrageous conduct constitutes an intolerable menace to the well-being of society. Let us clear out of the way any romantic notions of dare-devilry. This is nothing less than a sordid crime of violence inspired by vast greed. To deal with this case leniently would be a positively evil thing."

Charlie Wilson, Tommy Wisbey, Jimmy Hussey, Bobby Welch and Gordon Goody were sentenced to thirty years' imprisonment, Brian and Lenny Field to twenty-five years and John Wheater to three years. Ronnie Biggs was found guilty at a later date after a mistrial and sentenced to a further thirty years' imprisonment. It made for a total of two hundred and thirty-three in all.

These were obviously showcase sentences designed to send a clear message: if you take on the Establishment and fail, you will not like the consequences. Admittedly, Jack Mills, the train driver, had been punched in the head (*not* coshed, despite what the police propaganda machine claimed) and was said to suffer from headaches. But when compared to the sentence of George Blake, the spy who sent up to forty of his colleagues to their deaths and received forty-two years for it, it made a mockery of the British judicial system.

The compelling message these disproportionate sentences communicate is that the judiciary value money far more highly than human life. Thirty years for committing a robbery without a firearm was supposed to warn the public and 'discourage the others', but it had the opposite effect. In many quarters there was a sneaking admiration for the train robbers, and these outrageous sentences simply made them into national heroes.

This view was further compounded when, three months after being sentenced, Brian Field and Lennie Field had their sentences reduced from twenty-five to five years. This is amazing, considering that solicitor Field was the only person in the gang who knew the identity of 'the Ulsterman'. If it were not for his pivotal role, the robbery would never have occurred. The size of the sentence reduction suggests that some kind of *quid pro quo* agreement must have been on the table to warrant such mercy, from an otherwise merciless court. When the robbers appealed against their sentences they were told, in no uncertain terms, to get on with their bird.

Upon hearing the appalling news that his companions had been sentenced to thirty years' imprisonment, Bruce Reynolds and his wife Francis decided to flee his bolthole in Albert Mews, Kensington and head for the high ground in Mexico. It was not long before they were joined by Buster Edwards and his wife, June. Then, almost a year from the day of the train robbery, in August 1964, Bruce and Buster heard the news that Charlie Wilson had been sprung from Winson Green Prison in Birmingham. Apparently, three commando-like figures had broken into the jail, using keys to enter the wing, overpowered the solitary prison officer on night duty and led Charlie to scale the perimeter wall to freedom. The *News of the World* proffered the theory that he was busted out by a group of mercenaries, ex-Special Services, but the truth was more likely to be that Charlie had bribed a screw for a copy of the keys, and asked his old friends to come and get him.

As is usually the case with the Home Office and the prison authorities once a prisoner escapes, collective punishment was introduced by means of tighter security measures, such as more time behind the cell door, continuous oppressive observation, and a red light glowing in the cell throughout the night. This is what was imposed upon Ronnie Biggs in Wandsworth Prison. Although the thought of escape had entered his mind – how could it not, when he was serving a thirty-year sentence? – Biggs wanted to wait until the Court of Appeal had heard his plea against the severity of his sentence before deciding to flee.

After Wilson's escape from Winson Green, however, he found the regime and conditions at Wandsworth so intolerable that he applied to see the prison governor to ask him to relax the excessive security measures. As he would explain in a letter to Labour MP Marcus Lipton, the austere conditions were compelling him towards thoughts of escape.

In typically dismissive fashion, the governor refused his request and sent him on his way. As a consequence, on 8 July 1965, when Ronnie was walking around the exercise yard of the prison with four pals, a masked man climbed on top of the perimeter wall and tossed down a rope ladder. The screws immediately hit the alarm bell, but four prisoners managed to scale the prison wall and drop down into an adapted, open-topped furniture lorry with mattresses inside. The screws on the exercise yard attempted to thwart the escape, but other prisoners in the pay of Biggs prevented them. Ronnie and the other prisoners were then whisked away in a green Ford Zephyr. All ports and airports were alerted, to no avail.

It appeared that, whenever the Great Train Robbery seemed to be fading into obscurity, something newsworthy would occur that forced it back into the public consciousness again. The story was like a virus, going round and round, dying down for a while and then coming back with a vengeance.

With Bruce and Buster going loco down in Acapulco, Charlie and his family hiding in Toronto, Canada, and Ronnie Biggs travelling through Europe en route for Australia, and finally Brazil, the hunt for the train robbers had truly gone global. As a former long-term fugitive myself, I know only too well the relentless pressures of living under an assumed name and identity. The rents are extortionate, the day-to-day cost of living expensive, you are unable to meet with friends or to trust anyone else, and wistful thoughts of home frequently invade your mind.

Little wonder, then, that Buster and June were getting homesick in Mexico. Edwards was on the verge of striking a deal with DCI Tommy Butler at Scotland Yard when, in April 1966, he heard that Jimmy White had been arrested back in Britain. Buster decided to wait to see how long a sentence White got before brokering a deal for surrender.

White's trial was held the following June. After hearing evidence that his fingerprints were found on a copy of *The Times* stuffed inside a mailbag at the farm, the Flying Squad made sure that any defence submission of 'no case to answer' would not succeed this time. Unlike John Daly's moveable Monopoly board, Jimmy's prints on the newspaper gave the precise date of his presence – the mailbag had come from the train, and had been discovered in the robbers' hideout. There was no rebuttal evidence required. The jury found White guilty and he was sentenced to eighteen years' imprisonment.

This was just the fillip that Buster needed. The ludicrous prison sentences were showing signs of returning to normality. If the prosecution accepted he had played a minor role in the crime – say as a cleaner at the farm, hired after the event – he could, in theory at least, walk away with five years. Although it is claimed that no deal with Scotland Yard was ever struck, Edwards flew home to Britain in secret and handed himself over to Detective Chief Superintendent Frank Williams.

During his trial, held at Nottingham Assizes in December 1966, Buster claimed he had gone back to clean the farm after the robbery with Jimmy White. The jury disbelieved him, he was found guilty of robbery and conspiracy to rob, and sentenced to fifteen years. (Exactly half the prison sentence the original robbers had received during the show trial.)

Two years later, in late January 1968, DCS Butler and an armed posse of Mounties arrested Charlie Wilson in Montreal, Canada. He was returned to Britain to serve his sentence.

As for the mastermind, Bruce Reynolds, he came back to Britain as the cash was running low and was arrested at a hillside villa on the 'British Riviera', Torquay in Cornwall. During a protracted *tête-à-tête* with Tommy Butler at a London police station, the detective advised

Bruce not to go against the grain and to plead guilty, rather than being portrayed as a menace to society and enduring a show trial. Reynolds, for his part, had noted how not one of the train robbers had been found not guilty by a jury – and also, of course, how the police claimed his fingerprints had been found on two Monopoly tokens and a tomato sauce bottle at the farm.

On 14 January 1969, almost six years after the Great Train Robbery, Bruce Reynolds appeared at Aylesbury Assizes in Buckinghamshire in front of His Honour Justice Thompson. He pleaded guilty. When DCS Butler was asked what position Bruce held in the gang, he said, "somewhere near the top". Reynolds was sentenced to twenty-five years. The sentence – on a guilty plea, for a crime where no one was maimed or killed – was not only excessive but vindictive and unforgiving. Reynolds just stuck out his chest and trundled off to prison. He spent four years in the claustrophobic and submarine-like Special Secure Units, five years in HMPs Parkhurst and Maidstone, and was released on parole after nine years, in October 1978.

As for the most celebrated Great Train Robber of them all, Ronnie Biggs may have been little more than an ancillary worker compared to mastermind Bruce Reynolds, but he remained at large in Brazil for an incredible thirty-five years. Then, after suffering numerous strokes, he voluntarily returned to British soil in May 2001. At the airport, he was arrested and remanded in custody to Belmarsh Prison in southeast London, where I was awaiting trial for possession of an Uzi submachine pistol, having been set up by informants.

While I was being escorted to a social visit one day, I had the pleasure of meeting Ronnie. He looked frail, and could not speak as a result of the strokes, but he looked me in the eye and we shook hands. He may have been back in prison, but his strong, vice-like handshake spoke volumes. The obdurate spirit of 1963 was still coursing through his veins.

As a final shot across the bows of British justice, it is alleged that the relentless bloodhounds of Scotland Yard stayed hot on the trail of the three remaining train robbers who remained uncaught – but there has never been enough evidence to bring them to trial.

THE BANK OF AMERICA ROBBERY

24 APRIL 1975

Recently, I was interviewed by a female researcher from a TV production company making a film about getaway drivers. She asked me what would have been the perfect robbery I'd like to have participated in during my days as an active thief. Without hesitation, I replied that there is something gripping about robbing a vault containing safe deposit boxes; the excitement of having ample time to open rows and rows of strong-room boxes must be like Christmas for the professional criminal.

I have always been fascinated by the Bank of America robbery in Davis Street, Mayfair in central London. It's partly because it has entered the rich annals of British criminal folklore, but also because I wanted to know how the protagonists managed to rob a seemingly impregnable vault.

Admittedly all professional criminals, whether they are sophisticated fraudsters, burglars or robbers, are drawn to committing the 'Big One', after which they can put away their masks, gloves and tools forever and bask in the financially secure sun. The only problem is that, when the Big One comes along, many villains become so absorbed in the magnitude of the crime that they overlook the basic rules of criminal survival.

This is when mistakes begin to occur. And, as we shall see, it was no different for the notorious Bank of America robbers. Somewhere along the line they must have forgotten the golden rule: the perfect crime is the one that goes undetected.

In order to describe this amazing event, we have to travel back in time to 1975, when the world was beginning a period of long-lasting change. On a political level, Maggie Thatcher took her first step to infamy by defeating Edward Heath for the leadership of the Conservative Party. In the USA, Bill Gates was just launching Microsoft. Back home there was turmoil, as Lord Lucan was found guilty *in absentia* of the murder of nanny Sandra Rivett, a major tube train crash at Moorgate station killed forty-three people, and the Birmingham Six were wrongly convicted and sentenced to life imprisonment.

On a more uplifting note, this was the year that West Ham United beat Fulham two-nil in the FA Cup final at Wembley, Muhammad Ali beat Joe Frazier in Manila, and

Queen hit the big time with the release of 'Bohemian Rhapsody', dubbed by some the best rock record of all time.

But before all this, aspiring criminal Stuart Buckley was released from prison after serving nine months for handling stolen goods. Almost immediately Buckley began to look for work, and struck gold when his brother, a construction worker, unwittingly told him that a position had become available for a maintenance man-cum-electrician at the Bank of America. In January 1975 Buckley applied for the post and, to his amazement, actually got the job.

In the past, Buckley had gained a reputation among his peers as a quick thinking and reliable criminal. He was always on the lookout for new ways to steal property or cash and was basically viewed as an ideas man, someone who spotted a weakness or loophole in the security of a target and approached other, more resourceful craftsmen to commit the crime.

Buckley had evidently been part of a successful fraud team, one of whose members would enter a bank with a forged bank draft and ask to cash it. The bank then made a call to see whether it was creditworthy, but this call was intercepted by a bogus telephone engineer nearby who gave authorisation for the draft to be cashed. Throughout this scam, Buckley had performed well and gained a reputation as someone who could be trusted.

Not surprisingly, it wasn't long before he began to apply his knowledge and prowess to the grander idea of robbing a bank. He approached a former criminal colleague called Frank Staple (not his real name) to discuss the idea. Staple in turn made a meet with a criminal colleague, Jimmy O'Loughlin, in a pub called The Guinea in Bruton Mews, Mayfair, to debate the idea.

One of the problems prominent in their minds was, if they could pull off the Big One, how would Buckley shape up after the crime? It was inevitable that he would be pulled in by police investigators and put under immense pressure. Despite tentative misgivings about his backbone and resolve, both O'Loughlin and Staple realised this was too good an opportunity to miss and decided to proceed with the plan.

Jimmy O'Loughlin was born in 1943, to the less than salubrious council estates of Chelsea, west London. Such was his strict Irish Catholic upbringing that he soon absorbed the social values of hard work and discipline. He was particularly proud of his father, who worked hard to provide for the family, and had every intention to emulate him. At school he found that he was good with his hands and received top grades for carpentry. Not one to get involved in customary adolescent petty crime or thieving, O'Loughlin preferred to focus upon the future and looked forward to the day when he could really utilise his talents. Upon leaving school he obtained employment as an apprentice carpenter and restorer of French furniture, where the use and understanding of tools became invaluable.

Initially O'Loughlin found this work satisfying, but,

after a year or so, the combined effects of low wages and interminably slow progress made him disillusioned with the trade. He needed to expand his horizons if he was going to make anything of his life. It did not take O'Loughlin long to realise that personal progress and success were often equated with wealth. He knew he was not going to get far on his £8 wage packet at the end of the week, and soon embraced the boundless possibilities of crime.

His training as a carpenter had taught him to plan and prepare well. The golden rule of carpentry – "measure twice and cut once" – also applied to his new profession of burglary. He would plan a crime, and then go over the plan time and time again until he was content with it.

More significantly, he always worked alone. In his view there was no value in carrying a partner as it meant double the noise, double the risks and half the cut. He started out with housebreaking – not domestic burglaries in working-class areas, but the country houses and mansions of the English aristocracy. Not only did this slake his thirst for excitement, but it also acknowledged the massive monetary gulf between the affluent and the dispossessed classes.

As he developed into a successful solo cat burglar, his confidence began to grow until he was successfully taking on projects along the sun-blessed coastlines of Spain and France. As the rewards became bigger so did his ambitions. Soon he was sipping champagne and swallowing caviar with the elite.

One of the benefits of having an inside man at the bank who was not a cashier or manager was that, as a maintenance man, he had complete authority to be anywhere in the bank. For instance, it was not unusual to see him in the storeroom, backroom, behind the counter, under tables, on the stairwell – even near the vault.

After the first meet with O'Loughlin and Staple, Buckley was asked to provide them with an impression of the key to the front door of the bank. If he came up with this then they could take the plan to the next stage. Buckley obtained the key and sandwiched it inside a tin of Plasticine in order to get a sharp impression of both sides, and of the key's width.

Now that they knew Buckley was serious, he was ordered to make a mental note of the bank's procedure – from who did what and at what times, to where the cash was stored at what time of the day. During his weeks of detailed observation, Buckley noticed how the bank's managers opened the vault situated in the basement area between 9 and 9:15am every weekday morning. This was done by turning two combination dials, six inches in diameter, to the correct five digit numbers. For security reasons, the manager had the correct numbers to one dial while the assistant manager held those to the second dial. In order not to compromise the security arrangements, they both opened their combination locks separately.

Once inside the vault, a large, prison-like barred gate with a nine-level Chubb lock was then opened, which allowed the cashiers access to the trolleys which contained the money. The trolleys were then pushed out of the vault to the cashier's desks, to start the day's business; the vault was left open until the end of the day, when the manager locked it.

Also in the vault were row upon row of safe deposit boxes. To access these, a deposit box owner had to enter the bank on the ground floor level, descend a flight of stairs to the female receptionist behind a desk in the basement, and provide her with the correct details and signature before being allowed into the vault with a key to the internal gate. Buckley noticed that the receptionist always kept the vault key on her desk.

At the end of the day, when the bank was closed, he also noticed that the cashiers would repeat the process by pushing the cash trolleys into the vault and then take their banking receipts to the manager for verification. The vault gate would be locked and the receptionist would leave her desk to visit the toilet, in preparation for her tube journey home.

Over the months of further observation, the team decided against the idea of a straightforward burglary as it would mean breaking into the bank and deactivating the internal alarm system. Alternatively, they realised there was a window of opportunity to creep into the vault with a duplicate key between the times when the cashiers deposited their trolleys, the receptionist visited the toilet and the bank managers came down to the basement to close the vault.

But before they could even contemplate putting this plan into operation, they had to find a way to get an impression of the vault gate's key, held on the receptionist's desk, and then find someone with the skill to duplicate it.

John Le Bosche

The best key man in the business at that time was the legendary Leonard Wilde, also known as John Le Bosche, aged fifty-two. It was rumoured that he could take one look at a key and make an identical copy from memory. Moreover, 'the Bosche' would not work with just anyone; you had to have an impeccable criminal reputation before you could even talk to him. For this reason, he had reigned for a long time in the underworld and the gumshoes of Scotland Yard always found him elusive.

Basically, the way the Bosche worked was that you went to him with the impression of the key you wanted made. He would take one look at the key and know immediately the level of villainy that you were undertaking. Sensing that the key was pivotal to the success of the crime, he would ask for a percentage of the proceeds – say ten or fifteen percent. Alternatively, if the Bosche liked the criminal venture and respected the villains on the job, he would ask to be put in on it. This is what happened with the Bank of America robbery. O'Loughlin, Staple and Buckley had little option but to accept him as a member of the team.

The Bosche made the keys for the external back and front doors of the bank; Buckley tested them and they worked perfectly. Buckley then set about trying to distract the female receptionist in the vault foyer, so that he could obtain an impression of the internal vault gate's key. Over a matter of weeks, he slowly began to get to know the pretty receptionist. From her perspective, she thought he was like any other fellow trying to chat her up with small talk and subtle compliments. But one day he knocked her pencils on the floor; while she bent down to pick them up, he quickly pressed the key into his Plasticine mould and then, full of apologies for his clumsiness, helped her retrieve the rest of her pencils. The Bosche duplicated the key and, when the receptionist visited the toilet one day, Buckley tested it and found it worked perfectly.

Naturally, the most critical aspect of the plan was timing. Both O'Loughlin and Staple had to enter the bank unnoticed by the rear exit, hide, and wait for the all-important signal from Buckley. Buckley had to wait until all the cashier's trolleys were in the vault at the end of the day, when the receptionist visited the toilet, and then notify his accomplices. But every time they were poised inside the bank, ready for action, the receptionist would not leave her desk until the manager had closed the vault. After two aborted attempts, the team realised there must be a better way to rob a bank.

Purely from a professional thief's perspective, there was only one way to rob this bank. Once it had closed for business at the end of the day, the robbers could have entered the premises unnoticed like they did before, via the back exit. Once they had donned their disguises and produced their handguns, they could have wrapped up the vault receptionist, then crept upstairs and seized all the other bank employees, chaperoning them downstairs into the vault foyer and wrapping them up. Once they had bagged up all the proceeds from the cashier's trolleys in the vault – reportedly over £250,000, nearly £1.5 million in today's money – they could have let one trusted robber leave the premises with the money while the others began to smash open the larger deposit boxes.

Admittedly, time would have been in short supply, but a small, efficient and effective team of four robbers could have opened between ten and thirty boxes before leaving the premises. As a precaution, the gang member who left the bank with the cash, now secure in a nondescript vehicle, could have acted as an outside lookout. If, for some unknown reason, the bit of work came on top, the gang still had the added advantage of leaving via the rear exit that led into the secluded Three Kings Yard, where a vehicle would be waiting to whisk them away.

The overarching problem with the creeping method was that Jimmy O'Loughlin and Frank Staple were coming from a sophisticated burglary mindset. With all due respect, these were not professional armed robbers; they were glorified cat burglars who preferred to steal by stealth and low cunning as opposed to brazen robbery. But in my opinion they needed to recognise that this bank was begging to be robbed, not burgled.

But the team had embraced the notion that the best way to rob the bank was by burglary at night. They would enter the building with the duplicate keys and drill a hole in the vault near the combination dials, getting John Le Bosche to work his magic on the locking mechanism. In order to do this, however, the team had to overcome three obstacles. Firstly, they had to have complete knowledge of the bank's night security. This would mean many weeks of night-time observation in a relatively 'hot' Mayfair street. Secondly, the team would have to locate and examine the bank's alarm system. Thirdly, they would also require specialist drilling equipment and tools for the task.

To makes things easier for the team, Buckley applied for permission to work in the bank at night. His pretext was that he would not be in the way of the bank staff and could work without interference. When he managed to locate the electrical alarm system, the team found an alarm expert to enter the bank and look at it. He checked it over and stated that it was a simple silent alarm system, triggered when an electrical circuit was broken. This sent a pre-recorded taped warning that the bank was being burgled to both the police at Scotland Yard and the security firm.

The alarm expert said that he was willing to deactivate the system but, when the time came, he pulled out of the operation, claiming that he was working on 'other things'. Both Buckley and O'Loughlin were familiar with electrical circuitry, and agreed that they would be able to disable the alarm system prior to the robbery. The only snag was that there was now someone outside the team who knew not only that they were about to burgle a bank, but also its location.

The contamination of an otherwise sterile plan was exacerbated when the team had to make discreet enquiries about the best way to drill a vault, exactly where to drill the holes and what drills were to be used. Suddenly their tightly concealed secret was beginning to leak like a watering can. Admittedly, the team were not bragging about the project, but if it were to be successful there would be a sizable reward on the table.

The venture was further polluted when the team had to purchase special nine-inch drills, in order to penetrate the vault and reach its tumblers. They were not the sort of tools that could be bought over the counter at the local hardware shop, but specially toughened, extended drill bits, made for specific tasks. It did not take the brain of an Einstein to realise these drills would be used to commit a serious crime.

As if this were not bad enough, Buckley had bumped into an old criminal companion and could not resist mentioning the problems the team were having. When he outlined the position to Peter Colson – an active, grade-A career criminal from north London – the old face approached O'Loughlin and asked if he could join the team. Initially, O'Loughlin was livid with Buckley for talking to outsiders about what could become the crime of the century. But, on reflection, he was aware of Colson's criminal pedigree and agreed to let him onto the team. The way he viewed it, more members would be needed to work on the safe deposit boxes once they were inside the vault.

While all this was going on, the team were taking turns to watch and log the visits by the night security firm. The central difficulty was that Davis Street was not the sort of place where you could loiter, waiting for the Group Four security guard to come and check the bank. There was a nearby steakhouse which was used regularly, but apart from sitting in a parked vehicle on the one-way street, there was no comfortable observation point. (However, one member of the team found out that a nearby public lavatory was a frequent haunt of single men looking for a gay liaison. This helped to draw attention away from their criminal enterprise.)

After several months watching the bank, a pattern began to emerge where the security company would not check it until 9, 9:30 or 10pm at night, then again at midnight and again at 3 to 4am, when the cleaners entered the premises. The team found it incredible that the security guards started their initial checks as late as nine o'clock onwards. It was only when they realised there was a computer room above the bank, where the staff worked until 10pm, that they understood why. Although the computer room was separated from the bank and had its own access door from the street, there was also an internal door that led to stairs descending right to the heart of the bank, where the vault was situated.

The team realised that, if they could slip into the bank at six o'clock, providing they were not interrupted they would have a substantive window of three hours to work on the vault door and safe deposit boxes. They could position two lookouts on the stairs near the computer room to monitor both the noise of the drilling and also any suspicious activity emanating from the computer room, warning their accomplices if the situation arose.

On the day of their second attempt, O'Loughlin and another member of the team watched the bank manager lock and vacate the premises. As soon as he had disappeared from view, at 6:05pm, they entered the bank through the front door, heading straight to the rear to open the exit with their own duplicate key.

In the rear courtyard adjacent to the bank was a parked van with a roof rack and ladders on top. Signs on the side read, 'Sparkling Cleaning Company', but the van had been purchased specifically for the robbery in such a way that it was untraceable. Inside the van were six members of the team with an assortment of heavy drilling equipment and tools. Dressed in boiler suits, they quickly slipped into the bank. Two members were quickly dispatched to wait on the stairs leading to the computer room and monitor the office workers. O'Loughlin and Staple set up the electromagnetic press on the vault door and attached the drill; within minutes they were drilling into the vault.

This is a delicate process, as too much pressure on the drill makes the cutting edge of the drill bit overheat and become blunt. But they were making good progress when, after thirty minutes, the tumblers in the vault started spinning. They decided to leave that hole and start on the next one; once again, they were making good headway and were about five inches into the vault when a member of the team got overexcited and applied too much pressure to the drill. As a consequence, the extended drill bit snapped at the weld. The team had no option but to drill the tool out using a smaller drill bit.

When they finally retrieved the snapped drill from the hole, the men on the stairs came down and said that they could hear two office workers talking about getting a cup of coffee, debating whether to use the tea room near the vault or to fetch some coffee from across the street. All work stopped and the tools were bagged up, the team ready to flee the building through the rear exit. Then the office workers left the building through their own access door. Work began once again on the vault, and the men on the stairs were told to watch out through an upstairs window for the office workers returning. By now the time was 7:30pm and the team planned to leave the premises, with the spoils, by 8:15 to 8:30 at the latest, before the security firm made their first check.

The work stopped once again to enable the office workers

to re-enter the building. Then the drillers went for the home run. They were nearly six inches into the vault when the extended drill snapped yet again. It was close to 8pm and they had still not entered the vault. A quick meeting was called, as an urgent decision had to be made. Either the team continued with the drilling and overpowered the security guard when he entered the bank to carry out his first check, or they cut their losses and aborted the job. The danger with snatching the security guard was that he had to report in to his base after checking each building. If the controller at base did not receive his call, he could work out where the guard was from the last one.

With a heavy heart the team decided unanimously to abort the raid, packing their equipment and walking away, deflated but not entirely defeated.

Unlike their first attempt to rob the bank, this one would be noticed. There was a drill sticking out of the vault, and yet no sign of forced entry into the building. Later O'Loughlin learned that the bank had temporarily re-plugged the drill holes and were also to replace the vault door. All the external locks in the bank were also replaced, save the prison-like gate inside the vault. The only consolation for the team was that they had tried to rob the bank twice and no one had been nicked. All that the project had cost them was time, effort and expenses. (If they had treated the job as a *bona fide* robbery, however, they might have been ordering another bottle of Dom Perignon in the south of France.)

Understandably, after the second failed attempt the team dispersed. Their sense of disappointment was further compounded when Buckley paid a surprise visit to O'Loughlin. He told Jimmy that, when the specialists came to repair the vault, they said the gang were only a quarter of an inch away from the tumblers. Buckley also said that, although there had been a police investigation, he was not interviewed. With this near-miss in mind, O'Loughlin asked Buckley if he was up for another attempt. He said that he was, but they needed a new plan.

Thermic Lance & False Ceiling

O'Loughlin said that he had heard about a revolutionary method of entering bank vaults through the use of a thermic lance. This was a tool which burnt iron in an oxygenised environment to create very high temperatures for cutting steel and concrete. The only problem for the team was the noise and smoke that the thermic lance made. Buckley was despatched to check the air ducts at the bank, with a view to using the ventilation system to extract the smoke. Then the big breakthrough occurred. While he was rummaging around looking for the ventilation shafts, he noticed a false ceiling in the basement outside the vault. He told O'Loughlin, and together they came up with the idea of hiding in the false ceiling to monitor the bank managers opening the vault in the morning.

Buckley was sent back to the bank, to check the space

in the false ceiling and to see if it travelled right up to the vault. If it did, he was to make a hole in the ceiling to see if he could view the combination dials. Buckley came back with the exciting news that there was just enough space – about eighteen to twenty inches – to hide in, and that someone could lie down in the cavity and note the combination numbers as the manager opened the vault. He added that he had made a small hole in a polystyrene tile and could see the dials, which were fourteen inches apart, but could not focus on the numbers. This problem was quickly solved when O'Loughlin purchased a small Reiss telescopic monocle lens used by birdwatchers. When Buckley climbed into the false ceiling and focused upon the combination dials, he could see the numbers clearly.

The new plan was to make a reinforced wooden cradle inside the cavity of the false ceiling, so that someone small and light – like Buckley, who was five foot seven inches tall and weighed only eight stone – could hide in there all night until the next morning and successfully note the combination numbers. O'Loughlin reckoned that if Buckley entered the false ceiling before the first security check at 9pm, he would have a twenty-hour shift in the cavity before he could come down the following evening. Before they could do anything, however, Buckley had to acquire the key impressions of the external bank doors again and ask the Bosche to duplicate them. This took several weeks because the new Brahma locks were of a higher quality.

Armed with fresh duplicate keys to all the doors in the

bank, one evening O'Loughlin and Buckley slipped unnoticed into the premises. Buckley climbed into the false ceiling by removing a tile in the toilet. O'Loughlin heard him crawl tentatively across the ceiling until he was firmly ensconced in the manmade cradle. He had some water, sweets and a container to urinate in, should the need arise. O'Loughlin slipped out of the bank and left him to it.

The following morning, when the managers came up, Buckley had his powerful monocle telescope trained on the combination dials. As the first manager entered his five numbers, Buckley jotted them down. The next evening he came down from the ceiling and met up with the team to share his good news. He had obtained all the correct entry numbers for one of the combination locks. The same process was carried out again several weeks later, and the team were back in business.

Meanwhile, O'Loughlin and the Bosche agreed that it was best to use the same team as before. But Buckley was not happy about letting Frank Staple back in the team, as he had allegedly pulled off another successful job without involving him. In Buckley's view, he had openly welcomed Staple into his project when it was looking good, but the invite was not reciprocated when Staple found another bit of work.

This internal power struggle did not go down well with other members of the team. It was considered unwise and unhealthy to drop someone from the original team. O'Loughlin tried to reason with Buckley, but he was adamant that Staple was out. The other team members had no option but to agree to his demand as, with everything taken into consideration, this was Buckley's work. He had found the job, he was the all-important inside man, he located the alarm system, obtained impressions for the duplicate keys and the combination numbers to enter the vault. In effect, he was the kingpin of the whole operation. Without Buckley's input the plan to rob the Bank of America was a non-runner.

The internal bickering intensified when the Bosche heard that Colson wanted to bring two new members onto the team as lookouts. Le Bosche retaliated by asking to bring his grafting partner in on the team. To make matters worse, O'Loughlin could not stand the Bosche's partner and the whole project looked like disintegrating into a full-blown showdown.

Looking at the team from my point of view, this was not a unified group of professional villains but a deeply fragmented and suspicious group of individuals, all with their own hidden agendas. Perhaps the only unifying factor for the whole gang was greed.

These same dark sentiments were echoed by O'Loughlin's wife, Janet. She said that she did not like Buckley, she thought he was too clever for his own good, and that her husband should reconsider his involvement in the whole project. She added that she thought the robbery would go smoothly – but that afterwards he would get nicked and go to prison.

With these dire warnings resounding inside his head, O'Loughlin was still determined to press on. The fact that they were able to obtain duplicate keys to the bank, and the all-important combination numbers to enter the vault, blinded him to the dangers ahead. As far as O'Loughlin was concerned, this was the Big One – possibly the crime of the century – that would push him into the comfort zone of wealth and opulence. But in reality, he already had it all: a beautiful wife who adored him, a luxurious house in the leafy avenues of Surrey, and a seemingly bright future.

So what did O'Loughlin do? Perhaps to keep Buckley happy and focused on the task, he offered to go to work with him as his electrician's mate. His decision is still utterly incomprehensible, as he did not have to let all of the bank staff see his face. If Buckley fell over and spilled the beans after the robbery, all the investigation squad had to do would be to put O'Loughlin on ID parade and let the staff identify him. He would be boxed up like a gift to the British penal system, with a pretty red bow on his head. This was sheer craziness on the part of a man who had seemed, thus far, to be an intelligent master criminal.

On the other hand, however, O'Loughlin was showing some concern about Buckley's pivotal position on the job, going over his story with him in case he should get pulled in by the police. His underlying unease was reflected back by the rest of the team, when he suggested that Buckley should take a month's holiday before the raid to prepare him for the inevitable storm. But he was outvoted. They preferred that Buckley should return to work as normal, and put on a front to any subsequent enquiry.

After many months of preparing and organising the raid, the robbers chose Thursday the 24th of April to hit the bank. They were going to strike on a Friday evening, like the last time, but Buckley proved invaluable once again when he found out that the bank transferred the money out of the vault over the weekend period.

Prior to entering, one member of the team – a well-known villain called Billy Gear, from north London – was running late. He had been to the dentist with one of his children and the appointment took longer than anticipated. He decided to park his wife's red Ford car in Bruton Place, near Berkeley Square, but parked on a double yellow line and incurred a parking ticket. This was to play a significant role in his downfall.

Outside the Bank of America, Jimmy O'Loughlin watched again as the bank manager left the building and disappeared among the pedestrians. He calmly walked across the road and inserted the duplicate key in the lock, opening the front door. Dressed in a smart dark suit and corresponding briefcase, he looked like he owned the bank.

Once inside, he quickly made his way to the rear exit of the bank, using another duplicate key to let in the other seven members of the team. They were armed with small, powerful jemmies and large sacks to carry away their spoils. Once all the team were inside, they donned their balaclavas and gloves. Two men were quickly instructed to sit on the stairs to monitor the staff in the top-floor computer room. Then O'Loughlin went to the first combination dial to give the correct sequence of numbers. He did the same with the other dial, and then opened the vault door. As he entered the vault, the internal florescent light flickered into life to reveal several cash trolleys parked up in the middle, and several hundred safe deposit boxes of various sizes. At long last, their labours had come to fruition.

With an understandable euphoria and a rush of adrenalin gushing through his veins, he took the duplicate key to the internal vault's gate from his pocket and inserted it into the lock. He turned the key and *bingo!* – the door opened and the team poured inside the vault to wheel out the cash trolleys. They quickly bagged it all up and started going to work on the safe deposit boxes. They began to open them in rows; the first boxes were empty, but any disappointment was soon dispelled as others revealed a cornucopia of wealth and excess beyond all imagination.

Some boxes contained solely money, while others held priceless jewellery, diamond necklaces, bracelets, brooches and pendants, rings and watches, gold bars and coins, Krugerrands and sovereigns, plus banknotes of every denomination, from guilders to francs, dollars to sterling. This was the high watermark of the team's criminal career and they felt like kings for the day.

As more boxes were opened, however, a more sinister side of human nature began to reveal itself. They discovered several automatic pistols and numerous nude photos of well-known luminaries and celebrities, indulging in lewd sexual acts. Sometimes these were accompanied by blackmail letters which were not supposed to see the light of day. These were left in the corner of the vault for the super-sleuths of Scotland Yard to dwell upon. The team also discovered over £1 million worth of traveller's cheques, which they also discarded.

After opening a total of eighty-nine boxes they felt the weight of the sacks and were about to call it a day, when a man guarding the stairs said one of the office staff had walked down to the ground floor and was using the telephone. With so much now at stake, the team were taking no chances. Two of them seized the nineteen-year-old office worker and brought him to the mailroom near the vault. They quizzed him as to why he was on the telephone, and whether he had rung the police. Nervously, he said he was phoning the General Post Office's 'record of the day' service, to listen to 'Love Me, Love My Dog' by Peter Shelley.

A quick decision was made to return to the computer room and seize two other officer workers, one a female supervisor in her late twenties, the other a young male Indian computer operator who had begun work that week. Both were brought to the mailroom at gunpoint and trussed up with electrical wire flex taken from the bank's appliances. O'Loughlin made a point of checking the three hostages, providing them with water and reassuring them they would come to no harm, providing they complied with their orders.

One small but valid observation at this point tells us that, although the raid on the bank commenced as a sophisticated burglary, it rapidly transformed into an armed robbery with masked gunmen taking hostages. The team must have prepared for the possibility of having to seize the computer workers, but, despite all the months of detailed planning, they still forgot to bring handcuffs or other apt restraints.

It also reveals that the central organiser of the raid, O'Loughlin, was still thinking like a cat burglar. Anything to do with physical force or violence was anathema to him; he was not a robber, he preferred to steal other people's property while they were sleeping.

I had a heated debate once with Peter Scott, the notorious old-time cat burglar, who alluded to armed robbers as nothing more than thugs. Of course he had a point, but, speaking for the profession in general, I retorted that we at least walk up to our targets – frequently uniformed security guards – and take the money face-to-face, rather than creeping behind someone's back and stealing their personal possessions. Whatever the case, we are all unmitigated rogues and miscreants in the eyes of the law. But the professional armed robber receives longer prison sentences for being honourable and upstanding about his chosen trade.

Back inside the Bank of America, the team were ready to transport all the sacks of money to the getaway van in

Three Kings Yard, at the rear. At this stage, for security reasons, only two people knew where the spoils were going to be taken. John Le Bosche had arranged for a flat above a greengrocer's shop along South Lambeth Road to be used as the 'flop' (a place in which to divide up the loot).

Once O'Loughlin had checked the hostages, and told them to remain still until the bank's security guard showed up, the team left the building. Some went in the getaway van, others made their own way in vehicles parked in adjacent streets to the bank.

The getaway van reached the flop at 8:30pm and the other members of the team arrived a short time later. They pulled into the backyard and hauled all the sacks to the first-floor flat. Initially, after some money for expenses was pulled out, the banknotes were shared out into eight equal amounts for every member of the team.

The problem with the vast amount of jewellery was that its value could not be quantified in any honest or fair way. The best method the gang could come up with, given the time restraints, was to weigh the jewellery on the greengrocer's scales and divide it into eight equal piles, labelled one to eight, and draw corresponding numbers out of a hat. All the robbers agreed to this idea, save one – who wanted to pull out a specific £40,000 diamond ring for himself, though the others refused to let him. There was no post-robbery goodwill on this firm. However, luck was on his side as he picked the pile of jewellery with the diamond ring in it.

Another enterprising member of the team offered to buy his accomplices' jewellery for cash. Bids were offered, deals were struck, and the robber bought so much jewellery that he could barely carry it to his vehicle. All in all, the sharing of the spoils went on until the early hours of the following morning, when the team departed.

At 5am, the owner of the premises was summoned to burn all the evidence left behind at the flop, and was rewarded with a substantial amount of jewellery left in a large plastic bag behind a cabinet. He was now a happy man.

The crucial task for the team now was to stash their share of the loot away as quickly as possible. Billy Gear placed his in a safe deposit box at another location. Stuart Buckley's share was collected by a friend at a prearranged rendezvous in Fulham, and buried on farmland in the Kent countryside. Jimmy O'Loughlin had hidden his share in a secret flat he rented. Everything was going smoothly for the team; the bank robbery was planned so well and carried out with such military precision that it would take a minor miracle for the law to get onto their trail.

The first that Detective Chief Superintendent Jack Slipper, the operational head of the Flying Squad, heard about the robbery was on the morning after. He received a SPECRIM serious crime report through the police internal communications system from West End Central Police Station, stating that criminals had gained entry to the

Bank of America during the night, the vault had been compromised and safe deposit boxes ransacked. It estimated that over a million pounds worth of cash and property had been stolen.

Jack Slipper was born in 1924 in Ealing, west London. In 1941 he enlisted in the RAF. After the war he returned to his former trade of electrician for five years, before joining the Metropolitan Police Force in 1950. After pounding the beat in Brentford and Chelsea for a year, he was transferred to the Flying Squad where he remained throughout the 1960-70s.

Perhaps the highlight of his career occurred when he was involved in the initial arrest of Ronnie Biggs for the Great Train Robbery in 1963, and was later seconded to a special unit to track down the other train robbers. Slipper's proudest achievement, however, occurred in 1966, when he was part of the team that secured convictions for the Shepherds Bush police murders.

Undeniably, Jack Slipper was the proud owner of a distinguished crime fighting record. But, perhaps unfairly, his impeccable career will always be tarnished by his dogged pursuit of the fugitive Biggs. In 1974, Slipper received a tip-off from a journalist working for the *Daily Express* that Biggs had been found hiding in Rio de Janeiro, Brazil. Keeping the information to himself, he vowed to bring Biggs back. After an auspicious start, when the six-foot-three detective strolled into Biggs's hotel room and arrested his suspect, the plan to extradite him rapidly degenerated into a farce.

Allegedly Slipper was no great lover of bureaucracy, and had travelled to Brazil without notifying either the Director of Public Prosecutions or the Home Office. The plan was to let the newspaper get its exclusive story as Biggs was apprehended, and Slipper wanted to keep the whole caper secret in case the train robber should take flight again. But the detective's maverick actions caused an international spat, and the matter was taken out of his hands to be dealt with at a much higher political and diplomatic level. Henceforth, 'Slipper of the Yard' would be known as 'Slip-up of the Yard', and Biggs would be allowed to remain in Brazil – as his girlfriend was pregnant, and he was about to become father to a Brazilian citizen.

Upon receiving the report about the Bank of America robbery, Slipper immediately went to the scene and found the place in chaos. Initially it looked like the robbers had drilled their way into the vault, as there were scores of empty safe deposit boxes strewn everywhere.

Already, the London *Evening News* had run the front page headline, '£1 Million Mayfair Bank Raid. Gang walk in with fake key.' The newspaper added, "Six [sic] armed men using a duplicate key broke into a Mayfair bank last night and walked out two hours later with a haul believed to be worth more than £1,000,000."

Acting upon instinct, DCS Slipper sensed that there were not many teams of villains capable of pulling off a crime of this magnitude; therefore he contacted C11, the

Criminal Intelligence Branch of Scotland Yard. The primary role of C11 at that time was the collection, development and dissemination of quality intelligence to other Metropolitan Police units, such as the Flying Squad. In serious crimes such as the Bank of America robbery, it was imperative to get an early lead before the villains took off to their sun-drenched havens on the Costa Brava, or holiday resorts in Britain. Part of the role of C11 was also to log the addresses, haunts, current girlfriends and known associates of all top villains in the London area.

Slipper was relieved to hear that some weeks previously a senior CID detective had received a tip-off that a big bank robbery was being planned. The informant named the villains who were going to commit the raid, but was unable to provide the location of the crime. C11 had placed some of the named villains under surveillance but it had all come to nothing, until now.

Immediately, Slipper ordered undercover surveillance on all the named suspects – starting with Stuart Buckley and a well-known villain called Jimmy O'Loughlin, who lived in Kingston, Surrey. Buckley was the first to be apprehended, at the King's Head public house in Roehampton early that Friday evening, the very next day after the robbery. O'Loughlin was spotted leaving his Kingston home later that same evening with his wife, putting a large suitcase into a green Range Rover and driving off. The undercover surveillance team tailed him to Beech Court, Harroby Street, near Paddington Green, where he deposited the suitcase in a flat and drove off again. Then the police pounced, arresting both Jimmy and Janet O'Loughlin. They were taken to West End Central Police Station to be quizzed about the crime.

As predicted by the intuitive Janet, Buckley was being quizzed by detectives at a separate police station where he crumbled like the Twin Towers. Not only did the rat make a full and comprehensive statement, putting all the blame on O'Loughlin, he also gave up his share of the robbery, which was unearthed from a field in Kent, and offered to give evidence for the Crown.

Meanwhile, back at West End Central, O'Loughlin was refusing to admit to anything, claiming that he was at his mother's home at the time of the robbery. Assiduously trying to work out how the police had got onto him so fast, he sat it out until the next morning when two detectives entered his cell, showing him a statement signed by Buckley.

O'Loughlin knew from experience that the word of a grass was not sacrosanct in a court of law. Grasses were known to be unmitigated liars who would inform on their grandmothers to save their own skin. But four hours later, the same detectives entered his cell and proclaimed that they had found his share of the proceeds in the flat at Beech Court. Now the money had been found, O'Loughlin felt that he had little option but to cooperate with the police to save his wife from incarceration. He said that he was prepared to make a statement, but only about his own role in the robbery and no one else's. He was charged and, eight days later, remanded to Brixton Prison.

Later that week, both John Le Bosche and Billy Gear were arrested. Parking tickets issued in the Mayfair area during the weeks before and after the robbery were checked and cross-referenced against the named suspects; one vehicle led them to Gear, whose wife's car was given a ticket in nearby Bruton Place on the day of the robbery. The detectives found his haul from the robbery in a safe deposit box in Chancery Lane.

Nine weeks later, after several near-misses, the Flying Squad finally captured Peter Colson. They knew that Colson was using public telephone boxes in a specific area to contact his latest girlfriend, for whom he had a particular weakness. So, by the time the next call came through, they had surveillance on all the phone boxes and arrested him. Not one to give up easily, in the police station he made a bold attempt to jump through a window to freedom. He was so fast that he nearly made it, but the cozzers dragged him back by his trousers.

As for Frank Staple, he had slipped the police dragnet and was rumoured to have fled the country.

The Escape

As soon as O'Loughlin's feet hit the ground in Brixton Prison, he was thinking about the possibility of escape. For the most part of his adult life, he had employed his skills and intelligence for the purpose of breaking into places. Now the situation was reversed. But one of the main problems in being charged for such a high-profile crime is that the robber becomes the centre of attention. Fellow prisoners and screws alike all want a piece of him.

Doubtless initially, O'Loughlin would find it hard to lose himself in anonymity. The slamming cell doors and clanging gates would be a constant reminder of his loss of freedom. More disturbing to his peace of mind were the original informant who stuck his name in the frame, Buckley's rapid betrayal, the discovery of his share of the takings and his own signed police statement, all of which dictated he had to plead guilty at his forthcoming trial. Any strand of hope had been well and truly severed. It was these circumstances that conspired together to compel him to escape.

I went through these selfsame internal musings in 1983, when, at twenty-three years old, I was convicted of an armed robbery on a Brinks Mat security van and sentenced to fifteen years' imprisonment. As with Jimmy O'Loughlin, I was not going to sit in the spirit-sapping confines of a prison when I had the love of a beautiful woman waiting for me outside. Some villains look for an escape route via wheeling, dealing and squealing to their nemesis, the police. But more noble types – like Biggs, O'Loughlin and I – prefer to plan and orchestrate our own escapes.

Once your mind is set on escape as the only option, there are two vital rules to remember. The first is that it is absolutely imperative that no one else knows about your escape plan. Prior to the Bank of America robbery, O'Loughlin invariably worked alone. After the robbery, however, he had been grassed up by two separate individuals. He was not about to make the same mistake again. Secondly, and equally importantly, O'Loughlin realised that you only get one chance to make a viable escape bid, and so it has to be the best chance. There is no value in bold desperado attempts like that which Colson tried in the police station, as this only intensifies your security situation. With these central tenets in mind, O'Loughlin applied his intelligence and analytical powers to the goal of escaping.

The first point to explore was the prison itself. Prisons by definition are secure buildings, but over their years of incarceration many clever prisoners look for weaknesses and loopholes in the fabric of the building. As each flaw is exploited by the prisoners, so the authorities take measures to plug the gap. And so, by the time O'Loughlin landed in the echoing wings of Brixton Prison, the security was double tight.

The next focal point was the prison coach, the aptly-termed 'sweatbox' that transports a remand prisoner from prison to court and, if you are unlucky, back again. I have been in these old-style 1970s sweatboxes; once you step in the coach, there is a central aisle with small three-foot square cubicles and doors on each side of the aisle. Prisoners are locked in these for the duration of their journey to court. Perhaps the best analogy I can draw is with the confessional cubicle in a Roman Catholic church, the sweatbox being a small reinforced window that permits the prisoner to look out and watch the world go by. Once inside, the doors are double-locked and the prisoner is almost hermetically sealed within the compartment. The crew of two jailers will not open the cubicle for any reason, save an emergency which requires driving to the nearest police station to seek assistance.

But there is one other exit from the cubicle, an escape hatch at the top, intended for the occupant in the event of a serious traffic accident. The opening mechanism is situated at the front of the vehicle, to which only the driver and his colleagues have access. When I was at the notorious Ashford Remand Centre as a juvenile, once we had boarded and were on our way to court across London, we would rock the sweatboxes in unison and try to topple over the wagon as it negotiated a corner. This used to play havoc with the driver and the safety of the vehicle. Alas, we never managed to topple a sweatbox; I believe the authorities merely strengthened the vehicle's suspension system.

With possible escape from the sweatbox ruled out, O'Loughlin focused upon any weaknesses in security as he was escorted to the magistrate's court cells. In the Bank of America team's case, they were driven to Great Marlborough Street Magistrate's Court. The sweatbox would pull into a courtyard, surrounded on all sides by high buildings, and two large gates would be closed behind them. The prisoners would be released from the cubicles individually and delivered to the court jailers, who would be waiting outside the sweatboxes to escort them to the holding cells.

This process of transport to and from the magistrate's court would continue on a weekly basis until the case was ready for committal to the higher crown court, as magistrates have never had the legal authority to remand anyone to custody for longer than seven days. This suited O'Loughlin, as the regular monotony of returning to the court every Monday gave him the perfect opportunity to study the jailers, buildings and court routine for any defects or loopholes.

When he was being escorted from the sweatbox to the holding cells in the bowels of the courthouse, he noticed that the court jailers would sometimes wait at the bottom of the stairs. This might give him enough time and space to sprint across the small courtyard, scoot up some wrought iron stairs attached to an adjacent building and climb onto the rooftops. Once he was on the roof he could dart across several buildings and descend into the streets below, disappearing among the crowds.

Admittedly, this was not the best escape plan in the world. But, once O'Loughlin was up on the roof, being a fit, sharp-minded man in his early thirties, he knew it had a chance of success. The only problem was that the position of the courthouse jailers was unpredictable; sometimes they would wait at the bottom of the stairs to greet their charges, at others they would wait for them as they stepped off the coach. As previously stated, you only get one chance in the escape game and it has got to be your best shot.

The next area of investigation was the courtroom itself, or, more specifically, the dock where the defendants were housed. Defendants have leapt over the dock to escape a thousand times, and their success rate largely depends on several factors: the seriousness of the offence; the age and alertness of the jailers; how many police and have-a-go heroes are present in the courtroom; an intimate knowledge of the court building and escape route.

O'Loughlin's was a high-profile case attracting great media interest, with eight defendants crammed into the dock and a small army of sixteen-stone constables and detectives ready to jump on any defendant who made a dash for the exit. It would be tantamount to a rock superstar leaping into the audience at a live concert – the only difference being that the fans would adore the rock star, while the bogies abhorred the bank robbers. (I recall one dock escape incident where the counsel for the defence valiantly apprehended the defendant. No doubt he was on legal aid.)

As the weeks passed, the initial buzz of court appearances subsided into a monotonous chore. But O'Loughlin maintained a high level of vigilance. He made a point of being polite to lawyers and jailers alike, and tried as much as humanly possible to appear insignificant himself. With larger-than-life characters like John Le Bosche, Billy Gear and Peter Colson in the dock, this was not impossible.

One significant observation that O'Loughlin made was that solicitors and their clerks had the run of the place. Invariably, they would be up and down the court cells, interviewing prisoners, taking statements, arranging bail, checking and double-checking their briefs before any oratorical representation even began in court.

He also noticed that the court attendees would unwittingly slide into a social pecking order: those in the legal profession – such as counsel, lawyers and solicitors' clerks – were shown due deference and courtesy; the police would be granted recognition and respect; while the prisoner would be shown thinly veiled condescension and contempt. This gave O'Loughlin an excellent idea.

He noticed that, when he left the dock to return to the holding court cells, he passed through a locked door into the custody area, adjoining a long, narrow passageway to another locked door, which led to the holding cells. Also along the passageway were two other doorways, the first leading to the bail room and the exit from the custody area, the second to a toilet used by solicitors and their clerks. Upon leaving the dock the jailers would lead the way, escorting defendants and legal representatives through the passageway to the holding cells, with another jailer following up the rear to make sure the prisoners were accounted for.

Due to the large number of defendants and briefs leaving the courtroom it was quite a crush. Keeping his plans to himself, O'Loughlin decided that the next time he appeared at court he would dress very smartly, in dark suit, shirt and tie, carry a large number of deposition papers with the customary crimson ribbon holding them together, and, in the short walk back to the holding cells, slip into the lawyers' toilet and wait until all the others had passed – then walk back to the bail room and bluff his way out of the custody area and into the court foyer, posing as a solicitor.

The following week, as the defendants made their way from Brixton Prison to Great Marlborough Street, O'Loughlin was going over his plans. With a fresh, crisp white shirt, tie, sharp suit and new haircut, he looked every inch a lawyer. As Colson was handcuffed to a policeman due to his desperate escape bid from the police station, O'Loughlin offered to carry his legal depositions. Inadvertently this played right into his hands, as all the attention of the courtroom was on the defendant shackled to the oversized constable.

As the hearing terminated and jailers, lawyers and defendants shuffled along the narrow passageway, O'Loughlin nonchalantly slipped into the lawyers' toilet. He let all the others walk pass him and, once they were in the holding cells area, walked back holding two bundles of deposition papers, strolling purposefully into the bail room and up to the exit door. He said, in his best chambers voice, "Thank you very much," the prompt for the solitary jailer to open the door. As two genuine lawyers came into the bail room directly behind him, he gave them an acknowledging nod. The guard fell for the ruse and opened the door.

Straining to hold his nerve, O'Loughlin calmly strolled into the ornate atrium of the courthouse and headed directly for the exit. Once outside, he dismissed the natural urge to run and slipped across Great Marlborough Street, into Carnaby Street, and walked to Regent's Street where he hailed a black taxi, instructing the driver to take him to Kensington High Street as fast as he could. All in all, from bail room to black cab took three minutes.

He imagined the scene of utter chaos and confusion back in the bowels of the courthouse, when the jailers realised that they were one prisoner short – and when they had to disclose the news of the escape to DCS Slipper of the Yard. This was like the Biggs in Brazil fiasco all over again.

After debouching from the taxi at Kensington High Road, O'Loughlin jumped on a bus to Earl's Court. He knew that, by the end of the day, the Flying Squad would have retrieved his police and prison files and would be mounting round-the-clock observations and telephone intercepts on all his close family, friends and criminal associates. He needed time and space to think; he could not walk the streets, so he went to the cinema. Staying in tune with his predicament, he watched *The Wilby Conspiracy*, a film about two men on the run from the

Afrikaner police. In the picture house he scrolled through his mind's hidden files for someone he could trust, yet who was not known as a friend or associate.

He thought about contacting an old girlfriend he had courted ten years earlier. She was trustworthy and still fond of him, but they had not seen each other for many years. Upon leaving the cinema, the dramatic news of his escape was already blazoned across the newsstand billboards, with the *Evening Standard* exclaiming, 'Mayfair Bank Robber Escapes from Court'.

O'Loughlin quickly made his way to his former girlfriend's address. Once he explained the situation, she was only too pleased to help. She called her father in the Surrey countryside; he agreed to come to London to collect Jimmy. When they arrived back at his cottage at midnight, O'Loughlin was shown the spare room and fell into a deep sleep. It had been a long and stressful day, but his escape plan had worked.

Back at Scotland Yard, Jack Slipper and his bloodhounds were waiting to be unleashed. Slipper assumed operational control, as there were mutterings at the Yard as to how one of the Bank of America robbers could simply walk out of a secure courthouse in central London. He knew that the best way to shut up the cynics was to re-arrest his quarry as soon as possible.

The first task Slipper authorised was twenty-four-hour observation and surveillance of O'Loughlin's wife, who was still residing at their house in Kingston, Surrey. But Janet was young, shrewd and intelligent, and it was not long before she was waving to the detectives who followed her. She said she could always recognise an undercover, as he invariably wore a leather jacket and jeans. (It's still the same today, I might add.) In the end, Slipper realised he was not getting anywhere with her under observation and decided on another approach.

Slipper and another senior officer paid her a visit, feeding her the traditional spiel that it was in her husband's own interest to give himself up. He told her how life on the run was not a pleasant business, especially if there was not adequate cash available.

(I know from experience what it is like to be a prisoner on the run. In November 1984 I was Britain's number one fugitive, after escaping from a prison van taking me to Parkhurst Prison on the Isle of Wight. Fortunately, I had appreciable support from friends and enough funds to enable me to remain at large for nearly two years. Being on the run without either is like trying to breathe underwater.)

Slipper also spitefully added that, even if she did not take off to be with her husband, he would inevitably shack up with someone else. This was supposed to be the killer blow, as Slipper knew that she was fiercely loyal to O'Loughlin and they were obviously in love. But Janet was astute enough to see through his devious ploy, standing her ground and letting him waffle on.

In the meantime, O'Loughlin was at a serious

disadvantage. When the police had found his spoils from the robbery at the secret flat in Beech Court, they also recovered a small nest egg he had been amassing from other criminal capers. Now his first task was to secure some replacement funds, to allow him to flee the country. He managed to rake together £1500 and find refuge in a central London flat, but, at £500 per week with an ultra-nosey porter to boot, he decided to take a golfing holiday in Cornwall while more funds were solicited.

After two weeks gracing the greens and fairways, he caught the train back to Paddington and was given a room with friends of a friend in Edgware. By now he was longing to see his wife; a good two months had passed since the courtroom escape, so he decided to pay Janet a surprise visit. He slipped over the back wall of his Kingston home and entered the back door. She was elated to see him, but concerned about his safety and wellbeing.

(When I was recaptured after two years on the run, during which time my wife gave birth to our beautiful daughter, other prisoners would ask me why I did not flee the country and live abroad. There was one simple answer to this logical question: I never escaped to be free; I escaped to be with my loving wife and children. I believe the same sentiment applies to O'Loughlin here; it was the boundless love of a good woman that made his desire to escape so compelling that it ensured he succeeded. Now that he was back in the loving arms of his sweetheart, he wanted to keep it that way.)

O'Loughlin renovated the house in Kingston, constructing a hidey-hole in the cupboard under the stairs. He removed the two six-inch floorboards, cut the nails that protruded from the bottom so that they looked functional, cut a joist and made a snug cavity with enough room for one person to hide in. He also secured sliding bolts to the underside of the floorboards which secured the whole fixture. During a test run it took him twelve seconds to slip into the hidey-hole. He positioned the dusty carpet in the cupboard to fall into place once he was inside. It was the perfect miniature panic room, a domestic safe haven where one could sit out any crisis, such as a visit from the Flying Squad or violent intruders.

But both O'Loughlin and his wife knew it was a short-term arrangement. The undercover detectives were still following her to work and through the park where she walked their pet dog. They occasionally paid her a visit which, on the surface, was perfunctory and amicable, but on a deeper level it was a subtle form of harassment.

O'Loughlin's plan was to obtain a false passport, accumulate enough funds to slip over to France and drive down to Spain, where the unidentified Bank of America robbers who got away were residing. Obtaining the passport was the biggest problem. Although O'Loughlin had changed his appearance by growing a moustache and dyeing his hair, he did not like the risk of providing the passport office with a recent photograph of himself. Instead, for £1,000, someone who looked like O'Loughlin was prepared to let him use his passport. By the time it was all arranged, O'Loughlin also had £6,000 saved.

Various contacts in the London underworld offered to get him out of the country safely, but the fees were extortionate. One escape specialist wanted £10,000 for a safe passage to Brazil. Another wanted half that sum to secrete him in Ireland. O'Loughlin opted to travel second class and, for £2,500, arranged for a fishing boat to take him across the Channel to the port of Cherbourg in France. Once in France he was met by a friend who had driven over from Britain with his luggage. He pointed the Jaguar XJ6 towards Spain and motored towards the sun, sand and sangria

Two days later, after smashing the engine sump of the Jaguar and bribing two Guardia Civil to let him continue his journey, he arrived in Marbella on the Costa del Sol. He tracked down the villa where Frank Staple was staying, only to find out that he had been arrested two days earlier by the Spanish authorities as the British Home Office were seeking his extradition. (This was in the days before a firm extradition treaty existed between the UK and Spain. One day before Staple was to be extradited, the Spanish police had a change of heart and released him. He flew to Morocco, which did not have any kind of treaty with the British.)

O'Loughlin spent two weeks doing the rounds in Marbella, and then decided to save his funds and travel to the north of Spain to visit another friend. He was greeted with open arms and stayed for several months. But what he really wanted was for his fellow expatriate fugitives from the robbery to provide his wife with sufficient funds to come and join him. None were forthcoming. As his own finances dwindled fast, he was caught in the classic dilemma of poverty and pride. He could remain in Spain and live in the pockets of others, or fly back home to chase up some old favours. He decided on the latter option, catching the next flight to Gatwick airport. By the end of the evening, much to his wife's amazement, he was over the wall and back at their Kingston love-nest.

Drawing on personal experience, one of the biggest shortcomings of being a fugitive is the cost of living. I was paying £1,000 per month for a luxury basement apartment in Chelsea during 1984-1985. It was expensive, to be sure, but then what price do you put on your freedom? It's a case of either surrender, and forfeit your freedom, or dig in deep, get out there and earn some money. There are no other options.

O'Loughlin had a heart-to-heart with his wife and they jointly decided that, after the coming weekend, he would call the police and give himself up. It was a brave decision, though not necessarily one I would make in the same circumstances. I have found that sometimes it suits those around you for you to give yourself up to the authorities, as it makes their existence much more bearable. But it is not they who have to confront the harsh realities of long-term imprisonment: the loneliness, isolation, frustration, noise and offensive odours of hundreds of men living under one roof.

In my view, it goes against human instinct to volunteer for imprisonment; it is the most natural human impulse to flee towards freedom. Not that O'Loughlin had much choice anyway. On Saturday 10 April 1976, forty-eight hours before he was due to surrender, the old friend came to visit who had helped him escape to France. He arrived about 10pm and left thirty minutes later. A short while after he had departed, there was a resolute rap on the front door. Instinct told both Janet and her husband it was not the Avon lady calling.

O'Loughlin quickly slipped into the hidey-hole and locked the trapdoor. He heard the Flying Squad come into the house and begin a thorough search. Janet knew it was far from a routine spin, as they had a long pole with a noose attached to a Great Dane and crowbars to take up the floorboards.

It transpired that the so-called friend who had left earlier had, like Buckley, become a stool pigeon. Evidently, he was pulled in by the police and threatened with imprisonment for aiding and abetting an escape prisoner, if he did not cooperate. Naturally they found the hidey-hole and re-arrested O'Loughlin. To some degree, he blamed himself for this mistake. When he was on his way to France, his friend asked him where he was staying while he was in Britain; O'Loughlin unthinkingly told him about the inner sanctum in his house, not thinking that he was ever going to use it again. It proved a momentous mistake.

I do not know Jimmy O'Loughlin personally and have never met him. He appears to be a very genial and level-headed guy, but he must have been a poor judge of character as he was grassed up three times over: by the unknown informant close to him before the raid; by the milky Stuart Buckley after the raid; by a seemingly close friend who had come to his house and sat on his sofa. It seems as if the whole of humankind was conspiring to ruin this man.

I know what it is like for a person to come to your home, masquerading as a loyal friend while planning your downfall. I can empathise profoundly with the way O'Loughlin must have been feeling as he was escorted back to the south London prison. Treachery and betrayal appeared to be coming out of the walls. He did not know who to trust.

One thing is for sure. As soon as O'Loughlin was returned to HMP Brixton, he was notified that his security classification had been reassessed in the light of the courtroom escape, and he was now categorised as a category-A prisoner. Basically this meant he would be held in top security conditions at the jail, and all his visitors would have to be vetted by the Home Office. He was allocated to a Special Secure Unit (SSU) at the end of A-wing, allegedly housing some of the most dangerous remand prisoners in London – including the Bank of America robbers.

By this time, exactly a year since the robbery, the other defendants were almost ready to face trial. Solicitors and Queen's Counsels had been briefed, prosecution papers served and alibis put forward. Alas, much of the preparation for the trial did not affect O'Loughlin, as he was going to plead guilty.

In retrospect, O'Loughlin should have remained at large until after his accomplices had their trial. Not only could he have seen how the arch-traitor Buckley performed in the dock, it would have given him an insight into the verdicts and sentences being dished out. This in itself may have radically altered his decision to give himself up. Buckley may even have changed his mind about giving evidence in open court. For when the more insipid school of villain opt to give evidence for the Crown, they make very confident prosecution witnesses for their police handlers in the interview room, but, under the full public glare of the court, with an erudite counsel for the defence cross-examining them, it is a different matter.

On 10 June 1976, almost fourteen months after the robbery, nine men and a woman appeared in the dock of the Old Bailey to face a variety of counts including conspiracy to rob, robbery and handling stolen goods. The police claimed that they had found the flop where the robbers had their count-out. When scene-of-crime officers had vacuumed the carpet in the upstairs flat, they allegedly found traces of gold dust and a diamond tie pin.

An application was made on behalf of the prosecution

because, as only £500,000 was recovered from an estimated £8-£12 million haul, there was a real fear that an attempt would be made to nobble the jury. The judge, Alan King-Hamilton, agreed and the jury were give round-the-clock protection. This is never a good sign for the defence, as there is always the chance that the jury may become close to their protectors and this could damage the integrity of the verdict.

After all the defendants pleaded not guilty, save O'Loughlin and, of course, Stuart Buckley, the trial got underway in earnest. O'Loughlin was remanded in custody until after the trial had concluded. As a precaution, a junior counsel was employed to sit throughout the trial on his behalf, in case evidence was produced that may have supported mitigation during the sentencing process.

At the heart of the prosecution's case was the evidence provided by Stuart Buckley. Buckley had been pivotal to the whole operation. He not only found the target, researched and instigated the crime, he also dictated who was going to take part. Less than thirty-six hours after its success, he also began to bring the perpetrators to their knees. To some degree, he was the perfect participatory informant; he created the perfect crime with the perfect prize, and watched as all the other members of the team follow him over the cliff like lemmings. While awaiting trial he was held in solitary confinement at Wandsworth Prison for his own protection. Several attempts were made to nobble him but, when this did not work, he was attacked with chair legs and had the contents of a piss-pot thrown in his face. Every time he left his cell and was seen by the wider prison population, he was the recipient of unspeakable verbal abuse.

As the trial continued throughout the summer, it was not without drama. One of the defendants, by the name of O'Donnell, was blasted with a double-barrelled shotgun near his home in Finchley, north London. He underwent surgery and lost his left leg. Rumours circulated as to why this happened, putting it down to an old feud that caught up with him. The judge adjourned his case until after the trial and, on 12 December 1977, he pleaded guilty to conspiracy to burgle the Bank of America and was sentenced to two years' imprisonment, suspended for two years.

After a trial lasting almost six months, in mid-November 1976 the jury were sent out to deliberate their verdicts. They spent two nights in a local hotel and found the main body of the defendants guilty. Three defendants facing minor charges were found not guilty, including the wife of John Le Bosche. She nearly fainted.

The next day, His Honour Judge King-Hamilton QC listened to mitigation pleas before passing sentence. He mentioned the size of the crime, adding that it was beyond the parameters of what is considered "a normal crime", and that he had a public duty to pass sentence accordingly. More critically, he said that the trial had lasted six months and was a burden upon the public purse.

As for the considerable proceeds of the robbery that were still outstanding, he announced, "What has been concealed will remain salted away so far as you are concerned for a great many years. It is the duty of the court to ensure that the defendants will not be allowed to enjoy any part of this vast sum of money for a great many years." He then instructed the jailers to call the defendants one by one for sentencing.

The first were the perceived ringleaders. Leonard Wilde, a.k.a. John Le Bosche, received twenty-three years' imprisonment. The judge said that he would have received a longer sentence, but that the defendant's age had to be taken into consideration. Upon hearing the sentence there was uproar in the public gallery, and, throughout the remainder of the sentencing, it had to be cleared twice. Peter Colson got twenty-one years; as he walked from the dock he said that he hoped the jury would sleep well that night.

Next was Jimmy O'Loughlin. After hearing the judge pontificate about the defendants fighting a losing battle, he was given credit for pleading guilty at an early stage, and for showing some care and consideration toward the hostages in his charge. Nonetheless, he was sentenced to seventeen years' imprisonment. Billy Gear received eighteen years. Edward Jeffrey, Harry Taylor and Michael Gervaise got twelve years, three years and eighteen months respectively. As for the despicably reptilian traitor, Stuart Buckley, he was sentenced to seven years and released early in January 1978. Provided with a new identity and a new address, he disappeared into the ether.

So in the final analysis, why did such a spectacular bank robbery go so drastically wrong? I believe that, from the very outset, Jimmy O'Loughlin and Frank Staple had some simmering misgivings about Buckley's resolve under pressure. For that reason they wanted to keep the crime firmly in the realms of a sophisticated burglary, not an armed robbery, so that if the crime did go boss-eyed the resulting prison sentences would not be too severe.

Even O'Loughlin's wife had Buckley down as a slippery character. I remember my late mother warning me, as a child, not to play with two specific boys at school – not because they were mischief makers, but because she sensed that they were not 'right'. Later in life, both these boys became grasses. Janet too knew straight away that Buckley was a rat. But the others were blinded by the mesmerising lure of untold riches. It took a strong man to walk away from such a masterful crime.

The Bank of America robbers were not a strong and unified team, pulling on the same rope. They were a deeply fragmented group of individuals who, for the majority of the time, were more concerned with in-group competition and rivalry than shared objectives. Admittedly, O'Loughlin was the chief-of-staff and he tried desperately to keep the team focused on their goal, but some of the characters were too strong for him to control and greed took total hold. It is alleged that, even as the getaway van was driven to the flop, two large sacks of jewellery went missing. If this is true, then there was no hope for the robbers from the outset.

Even taking Buckley out of the equation, the preparations for the heist were fatally flawed. By the time the robbers committed the crime, an informant had already forewarned the Intelligence Branch of Scotland Yard that a big robbery was being planned and named some of the suspects. So who was that informant? In my view he was not one of the team, as he would have provided the police with more detail. A big clue lies in the immediate arrests of Buckley and O'Loughlin, suggesting someone on the periphery of their criminal or social circle. DCS Slipper had only received that particular information the next morning, and authorised observation of Buckley and O'Loughlin almost instantaneously. They were the only two robbers to be nicked on that day.

In any event, all the Bank of America robbers appealed against the severity of their sentences. (Le Bosche and Colson had their appeals against conviction refused.) On 24 February 1978, at the Royal Court of Appeal in the Strand, the Bosche's sentence was cut from twenty-three to twenty years, Peter Colson's from twenty-one to eighteen years, Billy Gear's from eighteen to fifteen years, Jimmy O'Loughlin's from seventeen to fourteen years, Edward Jeffrey's from twelve to eight years, and Harry Taylor's from three to two years. Michael Gervaise had already served his sentence of eighteen months.

It is believed that three of the robbers were never traced and are still at large. As for the elusive Frank Staple, according to DCS Slipper he was arrested at the port of Piraeus, near Athens in Greece. I have no record of what happened to him subsequently.

Lastly, in the long hot summer of 1986, I was still living the life of a fugitive in central London. At that time I was very close to a member of the Colson family, and had been told that Peter was being released from his eighteen-year prison sentence later that week. I had every intention to meet up with him and give him a coming-home present, which is the traditional way to greet a proper guy being released from prison.

The day before he was released, I robbed a security van in north London; as I screamed away on my powerful motorbike, I was rammed by a have-a-go hero and lost my lower right leg. I was charged, tried and sentenced to sixteen years' imprisonment. I never got to the homecoming party. Peter Colson had served eleven years of his eighteen-year sentence. I was just beginning mine.

THE SECURITY EXPRESS
DEPOT ROBBERY

4 APRIL 1983

This remarkable story starts on a bitterly cold Monday morning in the winter of 1982 – when a middle-aged businessman-cum-career-criminal, John Knight, was peacefully sitting in a Wimpy bar in Southgate, north London, sipping a cup of tea.

He was quietly minding his own business when, out of the corner of his eye, he espied the familiar yellow and green tones of a Security Express truck, making a delivery to a local bank. He noted that the crew had to wait for the bank to open its doors for business before they completed their delivery. Much to his disappointment, however, this was not a banknote run, as the courier company was delivering change, sacks and sacks of coins. As any professional robber will attest, trying to make a getaway down the High Street with weighty sacks of silver coins is, as we say in the game, a definite non-runner.

Unfazed by disappointment, Knight slipped his brain into gear and began to think on a deeper level. He realised that, due to the early scheduling of the delivery, the security truck must have been loaded up with the weighty coins over the weekend, and parked up somewhere where it might be accessible to him and his companions. The compelling image of breaking into one of these fortified trucks and stealing the money plagued him all day, to the extent that he decided to telephone Directory Enquiries, obtain the address of the depot in Curtain Road, Shoreditch, and visit the venue in person.

The history of Shoreditch is both colourful and grim. A built-up area situated to the north of the City of London, it either takes its name from Jane Shore, the mistress of Edward IV – who, according to legend, was disposed of in the eponymous ditch – or, more believably, was originally called 'soerditch' or 'sewer ditch', alluding to an ancient water course that ran west to the fens of Finsbury. In the latter part of the nineteenth century it became synonymous with poverty, prostitution and crime. This was compounded by the mass destruction of housing during the Blitz, replaced with high-rise accommodation and warehouses in the post-war period. Most significantly, Shoreditch was bang in the middle of Hoxton, Spitalfields and Bethnal Green, and a predatory criminal culture.

As John Knight walked down Curtain Road and surveyed the fortress-like headquarters of Security Express, he noticed that the multi-million pound, four-storey building was constructed like a prison – with all the ground-floor windows bricked up, electrically controlled gates, CCTV cameras and a twelve-foot high perimeter wall protecting an adjoining compound, where the security vans pulled in to deliver and collect their wares. All in all, the security depot looked impregnable.

But then an old cobbled alleyway down the side of the perimeter wall caught his eye. Alleyways had been his saviour in previous criminal ventures, and there was no reason why this one should be different. As he strolled down the alley he noticed an empty two-storey office block overlooking the security compound. He knew that if he could enter the empty office building unnoticed, he could sit at the upper window and view all the activity going on in the compound.

Later that day, under cover of darkness, Knight revisited the alley and entered the empty office building, replacing the lock on the front door so anyone could enter the building. He climbed up the creaky stairs and positioned himself at the window overlooking the security compound. It was perfect. Not only could he see the security vans in all their resplendent glory, and the back door leading into the compound from the main building, he could also see a cage where the vans backed up to steel shutters to load and unload the money.

Knight's excitement was almost uncontrollable, as he recounted his plan to steal the multi-thousand pound haul of coins to his companions. He was adamant that they were onto a winner. In order to garner more information about the day-to-day routine of the security guards and their vehicles in the compound, Knight's determined gang took turns watching the activity in the yard. They noted every detail about the shift patterns, changeover times, where the vans were parked, which way the CCTV cameras were pointed, even the weekly visits from the man who collected the shredded paper and the man who changed the locks on all the security vans on Saturdays.

More fruitfully, they noted that Wednesday was wages day – when money was taken from the vault, loaded onto trolleys and shipped up to the third floor for office staff to make up the wages packets. It was also observed how, on Sunday mornings, the guards would wash their private cars in the compound and let their pet dogs run around, and how they loved their morning cup of tea. They would open the rear door of the main building, wedge it up so that it would not close and lock them out, walk across the compound and retrieve a pint of milk from a purpose-made hatch in the gate control room. To the untrained eye it was an innocuous daily chore. But to the eagle-eyed observer it was a veritable chink in the compound's armour.

Initially, however, Knight's plan was to watch the security guards and vans carrying the coins on Monday morning. If they did not enter the loading cage and drove straight out the compound to make their deliveries instead, then the plan to steal the coins was on.

The overriding problem was how to break into the

Above: The police remove Royal Mail bags from Leatherslade Farm. Inside were the Great Train Robbers' combat uniforms, part of a goldmine of incriminating evidence.

Left: Bruce Reynolds, mastermind of 'the Train', faces trial at Aylesbury Assizes in 1969, after five years on the run. He received an overly severe sentence of twenty-five years.

Ronnie Knight is remanded from Bow Street Magistrate's Court to face trial for the Security Express depot robbery, after eleven years of voluntary exile in Spain.

Freddie Foreman enters the Old Bailey on charges relating to the Security Express job. Much was made of his connections to the Krays and the Great Train Robbers.

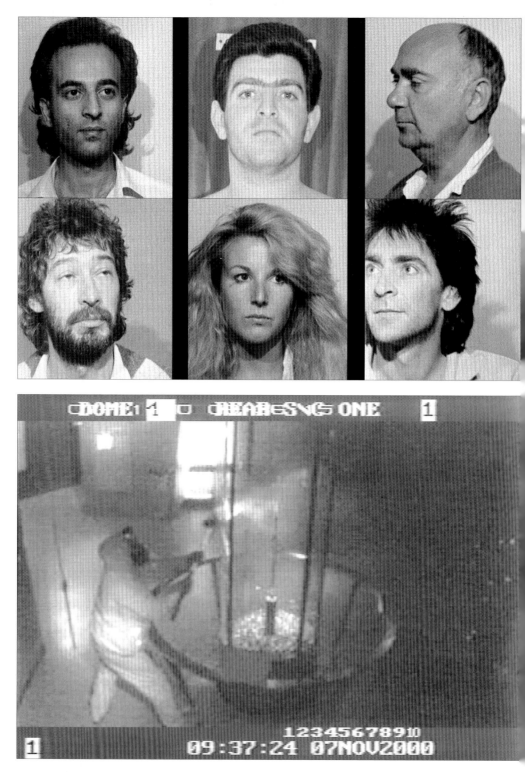

Top: The defendants in the Knightsbridge safe deposit centre trial. Top centre is the charming and charismatic Valerio Viccei, a.k.a. Gigi, seen in a more sombre mood.

Below: "I was twelve inches away from pay day." CCTV records Millennium Dome robber Bob Adams' assault on a De Beers diamond cabinet. In fact the stones were replicas.

locked security vans parked in the secure compound, without drawing attention to themselves. To resolve this dilemma, Knight sought the aid of a specialist engineer who made a unique circular cutting mechanism that proved productive when tested. The only problem was the noise the cutter made, and there were some valid arguments amongst other members of the gang as to whether the cutting procedure would be successful. With so much work already put into the project, it made John very angry. He did not want to walk away from the project with nothing to show for it, so it was decided to body-swerve the scheme away from stealing the coins and go for the lottery-size jackpot in the vaults.

Various ideas were put forward by the gang as to how they could enter the building, dubbed 'Fort Knox', wrap up the employees and empty the vault. One was to enter via the roof and descend the stairs to the main control room. Another was to enter via the fire escape outside the building, and another to ambush the locksmith when he changed the locks on the security vans at the weekend. Then someone mentioned the solitary security guard who left the confines of the main building to fetch the pint of milk from across the compound.

The plan was simple. Two members of the gang would penetrate the perimeter wall and test a possible CCTV blind spot in the compound, before the actual raid. If this was successful then the raid was on, and various vehicles and equipment would need to be purchased. Knight estimated that the gang would need two large double wheel-based vans (one painted in similar colours to the Security Express vans), two back-up cars, ladders for the wall, sticky tape and rope to blindfold and secure the guards – plus, of course, the obligatory shotguns.

All was going well, until a meeting between some of the gang in March 1983, at Jimmy Knight's scrap yard in Dalston, was interrupted by the Drugs Squad. The place was already under surveillance, as the Knights had a serious pedigree. (As well as John, Jimmy was also brother to the more notorious Ronnie.)

Upon seeing five well-dressed, middle-aged men enter the yard, the undercover surveillance team wrongly thought that there was some illegal activity going down. To the squad's disappointment there were no drugs or money to be found, but they took down the names of all those present. They were Jimmy Knight, scrap metal dealer, John Knight, garage owner, Terry Perkins, a property developer, John Mason, a launderette owner, Ronnie Everett, a publican, and Billy Hickson, who gave a false name. During the subsequent search of the premises, police found some specialist glassware that could be used in manufacturing drugs, and arrested Jimmy. (He was later acquitted of all charges.)

Then, in the night-time gloom of Sunday the fourth of April, with the City of London dead to the world until Tuesday morning, the first day after the bank holiday weekend, some of the gang went over the wall of the Security Express depot. The object was to hide in the shadows behind the dustbin area of the compound and patiently wait, until the night watchman, David Howsam, was replaced at 7am by the day-shift supervisor, Greg Counsel. The gang knew a lot of things about the Security Express workforce, and one of them was their almost slavish addiction to a cup of tea. As Confucius was wont to say, "He who makes tea solves problems." But in this case, the security men's regularity of habit would solve a problem for the men who came to rob them.

There was a skeleton staff of only eight employees due in that day, an 'elastic shift' designed to cope with only a handful of special deliveries. As Counsel trundled across the compound to collect a bottle of milk, he was ambushed by several men wearing masks. He was quickly ushered into the main building and told to keep his head down. Once inside, the robbers placed sticky tape over his eyes and bound his wrists.

This was the start of a four-hour nightmare ordeal. He was forced to sit at the main control desks facing the glass partition that oversaw the main entrance to the reception area. Underneath the desk were two masked villains with shotguns pointed directly at Greg's bollocks. He was told to keep looking down at the desk and, as his fellow employees entered the building, to let them in through the airlock entry system.

Then, one at a time, the employees came through the

electronically controlled airlock. As soon as they entered the main control room, they were seized by armed masked men and frogmarched to the security guards' locker-rooms, where they were quizzed about their official duties for the day ahead. Some were drivers, due to leave the depot to carry out collections at a nearby cash-and-carry in Hackney.

But the most valuable employees were the custodians of the vault. The first of these, Alan Grimes, arrived at 2:15pm He was quickly marched to a secluded room, where the robbers retrieved one key to the vault and the combination numbers from his wallet. They knew that there were two sets of keys and two sets of combination numbers; the custodians carrying these were called 'number one' and 'number two man'. Grimes was 'number two'.

At 2:30pm the 'number one man' arrived, sixty-year-old James Alcock. He had been the unfortunate victim of four armed raids in the past, and was probably looking forward to an easy and uneventful day. Moreover, he was not normally 'number one', having swapped shifts at the last minute. He had neither the key to the vault (left by the previous custodian in a brown envelope in the reception area) nor the combination numbers on him, so he decided to play dumb, which only antagonised the robbers. This was not a clever move. For they then doused Alcock with petrol, and threatened to turn him into a human torch if he did not cough up the key and the combination numbers.

By now, after nearly eight hours patiently waiting for the custodians to arrive, the tension was rising. Calls were coming in from irate customers wanting to know when their collections were due, the bogus Irish accents adopted by the robbers had subsided into out-and-out cockney, and Alcock kept giving them grief over the remaining key to the vault and the combination. It wasn't until they poured petrol over his left trouser leg and rattled the box of matches that he told the robbers where the missing key and combination numbers were hidden.

Leaving Alcock behind, the robbers grabbed hold of 'number two man' Grimes and escorted him to the vault in the basement. The main control room's vault alarms had been switched off, and now it was up to Grimes to open the vault. He carefully entered the combination numbers and spun the two heavy dials in turn, unlocking the vault with the keys and spinning the big heavy wheel to release the locking mechanism. He pulled back the thick steel vault door and it swung open.

At first the robbers were disappointed, as all they could see was darkness. Grimes then unlocked another grille facing them and switched on the fluorescent lights. As they flickered into life it was like a surreal dream, as the robbers recognised the familiar green canvas sacks replete with cash, in nearly forty cages.

Many were the times they had run across the pavement to accost a security guard, delivering the maximum £25,000 to a bank. Now they were in the mother of all banks, and an affluent retirement beckoned. No more stealing vehicles for robberies, no more going over escape routes, no more trusting the untrustworthy, no more sweaty palms and butterflies before the action starts. This was the beginning of a new chapter in their lives. And for their sheer audacity, they deserved it.

It took thirty minutes to empty the vault, including the seven safes on time locks at the rear. The time locks were already deactivated as the custodians were expected to come in that day. The gang pushed the money-laden trolleys out of the vault, over to the steel shutters and up the ramp, loading them into their own waiting vans. At approximately 3pm the robbers said their farewell speech to the security guards, all still tied up, promising them money in the post. With that, they opened the electronic gates in the compound and drove out. It had been a long day and it was not over yet.

After a while, the security guards realised that they were alone and struggled free from their constraints. They tried desperately to find a working telephone, as most of them had been sabotaged. When they finally got through to the police they settled down and cracked open bottles of cherry brandy and Martini left over from the Christmas party, to settle their nerves.

Detective Chief Inspective Peter Wilton of the Flying Squad, based at Walthamstow, had been called back from a family reunion in Somerset. By the time he arrived at the crime scene it was complete mayhem. The press and media had all been tipped off about the spectacular raid, joining the throng of local police constables, photographers and forensic officers who were collecting witness statements, searching for clues and fingerprints.

Almost immediately, the DCI suspected that it was an inside job. What professional gang of robbers would venture into a seemingly impenetrable building blind? From the very outset, he decided to keep an open mind and wait to see what came out of this organised mess. One thing was for sure: if the senior detective could solve this case it would become the highlight of his career, inevitably leading to promotion.

On Tuesday 5th April, the Commander of the Flying Squad, Frank Cater, briefed a team of sixty detectives at City Road police station. He made it plain to all that this was a major enquiry and that it was imperative to catch the villains.

Preliminary findings suggested the robbers had overpowered a solitary guard and waited patiently for another seven employees to enter the building. As the guards entered they were blindfolded, gagged and placed inside a storeroom. The robbers were incredibly civil towards their captives, using their first names, making them tea and rolling them cigarettes, even placing clothes underneath them for comfort and massaging one guard's limbs because of poor blood circulation.

Things only turned nasty when James Alcock refused to divulge where the key was, and the combination numbers to the vault. But what really intrigued the detectives was how the gang appeared to have intimate knowledge of the shift patterns, but not the most recent changes to the rota. Also, they knew that the top lock on the vault was called 'number one' and the bottom lock was 'number two'. More strikingly, the robbers even seemed to know about the secret panic button in the vault.

All this pointed to an inside job for Wilton. There were also some scuffle marks on the outside of the perimeter wall, which suggested that was where the robbers had climbed over, and a cigarette butt found in the toilet. Other than that, there were no facial identifications, no fingerprints, nothing. In short, the Flying Squad was looking for a highly professional gang of armed robbers with cockney accents and loads of money.

The first task the detective set himself was to obtain all the files on the previous armed attacks on Security Express vehicles. For he believed that, if there was a mole on the firm, he or she may have had a tickle before the big one came along. Secondly, there was a massive £500,000 reward put up by Lloyd's of London which he hoped would loosen a few tongues in the underworld. Thirdly, there were only a select number of armed villains capable of a robbery of this magnitude, and he wanted them put under close surveillance. There was no point in going round smashing doors purely on a hunch. It was far better to play the waiting game, as the robbers themselves had done, and to see who started spending and bringing attention to themselves. It was to prove a wise decision.

The double wheel-based Ford Transits, carrying nearly five tons of cash, grumbled and groaned as they powered their way up through Dalston, Stoke Newington, Tottenham and Enfield, to the relative safety of a barn in Hertfordshire. The journey had taken forty minutes in the safety of a convoy. Now they began to cut the canvas sacks with garden shears and empty their contents into large Hessian sacks.

The plastic and paper wrappings were put into a separate sack, ready for burning. Their clothes, ladders, rope, tape and anything else associated with the robbery was tossed into an old horse box, for disposal later. The yellow Ford Transit was as hot as mustard, but that would be chopped up for scrap metal in the coming days. At the barn, for insurance purposes, the money was split into two halves – in case one half was lost or discovered by the police – and several members of the gang departed with their share. Before they drove away, John Knight advised them not to do anything silly and not to behave like millionaires. The last thing he wanted was someone getting envious and ringing the bogies at Scotland Yard.

It was 8pm and time was moving fast. John still had to get the remaining half of the money to a safe place. He had made tentative plans to take it to a female friend's secluded house for counting, but this had fallen through at the last minute. Rather hastily, Billy Hickson and Terry Perkins had loaned a lock-up garage in Waltham Abbey from a fellow called John Horsley, who ran a car repair business called Alpine Motors in Dalston. They transported their half of the money from the barn to the garage and left it there for safety. The idea was to find somewhere safe to count the money, add the total to the other half of the proceeds, and then share it out equally amongst the gang. The quicker this was done the better.

John Knight had a business partner called Alan Opiola; together they owned a car repair garage called M&M Bodyworks in Southgate. But Alan and his wife Linda were more than business associates; close friends of John and his wife, Diana, they would frequently visit local pubs and restaurants together. John asked Alan if he could borrow his house for the day to count out the money. Alan said yes. He even agreed to hire a white Bedford van, so John could transport the money from Horsley's lock-up garage in Waltham Abbey to his house.

On the day of the count-out, Linda and her mother were sent out for the day while John, Terry and Alan set about counting the money. Sometime during the count-out, Alan was dispatched to purchase some suitcases for the money and, when he came back, was confronted with a mountain of cash in his bedroom, four feet high by five feet wide. John said he would never see that amount of money ever again. The money was counted, and Alan was given £25,000 for his services. That should have been the end of the saga.

Meanwhile, Billy Hickson was looking for somewhere to stow his part of the money. He was very close to John Horsley, and allegedly asked him if he knew anywhere he could stash his cash. Horsley obliged and hid it in his elderly father-in-law's flat on the same housing estate, in a secret compartment in an airing cupboard.

After a week or so, the vehicles used in the raid were destroyed and the money was counted and shared out. The press headlines were proclaiming that professional robbers had escaped with a fortune of £7 million, but the real figure was close to £6 million. Whatever the case, **fourteen robbers had shared £400,000 each between them** and now it was time to lay low.

As for the Flying Squad investigation, they were getting leads, but not the right ones. One of the overriding problems was the large reward of £500,000 for the capture and conviction of the culprits, as all sorts of nutcases were calling the hotline with seemingly pertinent information about the raid.

As the days turned into weeks and the weeks turned into months, the elite squad were getting nowhere. They had one minor breakthrough when they arrested a garage proprietor from Essex with £3000 in one pound notes, allegedly taken during the robbery. He was sentenced to eighteen months in prison, suspended for two years.

Then an expatriate working in a hotel in Saudi Arabia claimed to have been offered detailed floor plans of the Security Express depot. This proved groundless. And then, eight months after the raid, the squad decided to arrest Greg Counsel, the depot supervisor at the time of the robbery. This was based upon an unsubstantiated hunch, as he had given the *Sun* newspaper an exclusive account of the robbery against company advice soon after the raid. The police raided his home in Catford, south London, and found an old army revolver. He was arrested and charged, to bring pressure upon him, but later given an absolute discharge. Understandably, this left a nasty taste in his mouth, and Counsel would not be called to give evidence at any of the trials.

More productively, the Flying Squad had several known professional armed robbers under surveillance. One of them, Billy Adams, was followed for several months. During the course of the observations, Adams and his gang were spotted following Post Office cash vans out of the main sorting depot at Whitechapel, east London. A major enquiry was instigated, called Operation Nab. After several months of no action by the gang, the police felt that they had enough evidence to arrest and charge the gang with conspiracy to rob. Billy Adams was put on trial and convicted. Remarkably, he was sentenced to eighteen years' imprisonment.*

Meanwhile, the Flying Squad had an anonymous telephone tip-off stating that the people who committed the Security Express robbery were meeting in the Albion, a rundown old pub in Dalston, east London, mainly

---

*While he was in HMPs Frankland and Long Lartin, I met Billy Adams and we became close friends. Bill was one of the best people I served time with, an absolute breath of fresh air.

frequented by local crooks and rogues. The informant added that up to two or three of those responsible for the robbery were socialising with a local garage owner called John. The Flying Squad had many calls like this before, and had acted upon them, but this one needed checking. On 1st June 1983, an observation post was found outside the pub that also overlooked the local garage. The surveillance team of two would arrive early in the morning and leave late at night, noting anything relevant and taking photographs to corroborate it.

Over the course of time they found that the owner of Alpine Motors, John Horsley, was frequently visited by two smartly dressed men. The first one was Billy Hickson, who they followed to his house, a well-known convicted armed robber. The second mystery man took several months to track down. He was eventually followed to his house in Enfield and identified as Terry Perkins, a property developer. He was driving a Ford Granada which was registered to Alan Opiola's garage in Southgate. Undercover surveillance officers visited the garage and discovered another Granada, registered to John Knight of High Trees, Wheathampstead, Hertfordshire.

Although there was no evidence that these suspects had committed the Security Express robbery, the detectives surmised that their luxury homes, vehicles, attire and regular spending habits in the Albion pub all pointed to one thing: grade-A villainy. As a result, they would follow Knight, Perkins and Hickson around for weeks.

As can be imagined, pressure on the Flying Squad for a breakthrough regarding the robbery was coming to the boil. This was increased by a similar armed raid at a Brinks Mat warehouse near Heathrow Airport in November the same year. Once again, it was an early morning raid by cockney robbers, petrol was poured on a security guard and it had all the indications of an inside job.

In traditional Flying Squad fashion, the head of the Security Express enquiry decided to let the observations run over the festive and New Year period of 1983/84, to see if any new leads came to light. Sometime in the New Year, when a vehicle found near Horsley's garage was suspected to have been used in the Brinks Mat robbery, it gave the Flying Squad the perfect excuse to strike.

On Friday 21st January 1984, they arrested John Horsley and raided his house and garage, the Albion public house, a scaffolding yard run by his partner and Jimmy Knight's scrap yard nearby. They threw him in a police cell and asked him how, having been on the brink of bankruptcy in early 1983, he was able to buy two new vehicles for him and his wife, take a holiday to Greece, have double glazing fitted to his house, pay off his debts and still have £6000 in the bank by summer 1984. He did not have an answer. Or rather, he said he had done someone a favour and loaned them his lock-up garage. Once this opened the floodgates, he admitted to knowing Billy Hickson, Terry Perkins and John Knight, granting them access to his lock-up, loading a white Bedford van with sacks of money days after the robbery, and allowing Hickson to stow some of the proceeds in a secret compartment at his elderly father-in-law's address.

This was the breakthrough the enquiry required. The detectives promptly raided Horsley's father-in-law and confiscated £288,000 in cash. Around the same time, they swagged in Hickson, Perkins and Knight. Horsley made a full and comprehensive statement and offered to give evidence for the Crown. He was allowed a personal visit from his wife in the police station, but later refused to turn Queen's Evidence. He pleaded guilty at the trial, but his statement could not be used against anyone else involved in the case.

As a consequence of Horsley's confession, Hickson and Perkins were arrested. The police found £10,000 in cash at Perkins' address and he was charged with the robbery. John and Diana Knight were arrested the next day. The detectives found a piece of paper in her handbag with details of cash deposits to banks and building societies, totalling almost £250,000. Knight, Perkins and Hickson were remanded in custody.

More damagingly, in Horsley's statement he mentioned that John Knight, Terry Perkins and Billy Hickson had hired a white Bedford van to move the money. A shrewd detective cold-called all the van hire businesses in the north London area until he came up with a Bedford van at Kenning's Van Hire in Palmers Green. It was hired in the name of Alan Opiola, of M&M Bodyworks in Southgate.

On Wednesday 8th February 1984, Opiola was arrested, and for John Knight at least the case was blown. Opiola admitted hiring the van, using his house to count the money and purchasing the suitcases to transport it. He made a detailed eighty-page statement, also implicating Jimmy Knight in trying to organise an alibi for his brother.

Opiola was charged with handling stolen money and remanded in police custody under the witness protection scheme. Along with his wife, Linda, Opiola opted to give evidence for the Crown. When John received a copy of Opiola's weighty statement in prison, it was like plunging a knife into his heart. Both John and Diana had viewed Alan and Linda as loyal and trusted friends. Little did they know that the Opiolas would, when pressurised, exhibit a low cunning in order to survive.

Not content with the wave of arrests, the Flying Squad wanted to send a firm message to the Knight family against interfering with potential witnesses. This came about due to Horsley's sudden retraction of his evidence to the Crown. The Flying Squad did not want this happening to the Opiolas, so they embarked upon a second wave. They swooped on Jimmy Knight, Diana Knight, Diana's brother Albie, and her son and his girlfriend. These arrests centred on Opiola telling the police that Jimmy had arranged for Diana's son to go to Spain, to clear out his father's safe deposit box.

Jimmy Knight, Diana and her son were charged with perverting the course of justice. Jimmy was remanded in custody. Additionally, John Mason and Ronnie Everett were also pulled in over the alleged scrap-yard meet before the robbery. The reason they were there, they claimed, was to rent out part of the yard to run an American-style car auction. They were released without conditions.

The police also raided the Fox public house in Kingsland Road, Dalston, and uncovered a hardboard partition deep in the cellar. The uniquely damp smell in the cellar, so the police claimed, was very similar to that of the banknotes found at Horsley's father-in-law's flat. They even brought three cashiers from a building society in Mare Street, Hackney – where Hickson had deposited £30,000 – to compare the smell to that of the banknotes deposited there. The cashiers said it was similar, but this was far from scientific evidence. The police, however, were certain that some of the proceeds from the robbery had been stored there. By the time they raided the pub, however, the previous owner, Clifford Saxe, had sold up, banked £287,000 and bought himself two villas in Spain. He was another one on their 'to speak to' list.

After the defendants had spent over a year on remand, the trial started on 18th February 1985. In the hot seat was His Honour Judge Richard Lowry QC. The prosecutor was Michael Worsley QC, and the jury were given twenty four-hour police protection. The central planks of the Crown's case were the sudden and inexplicable wealth amassed by the defendants, coupled with evidence from main prosecution witness Alan Opiola that put the principal defendants at the count-out shortly after the robbery.

The north London motor trader explained how he stared in disbelief when he saw the row of banknotes stretching across a bedroom floor the day after the robbery. "Take a look at this, Al," he was told. "You'll never see so much money in your house again – and that is only a third of it."

The jury were told about the meeting at the scrap yard before the robbery; how the robbery was ruthlessly executed; how some of the money was counted out; how some was stored in suitcases for laundering in high street banks; how some was hidden in the secret compartment of an unsuspecting pensioner's flat, and how some was spirited away to Spain by those yet to face trial.

In my view, the most damaging evidence not only included the personal account by Opiola, but also the £288,000 found in the secret compartment and linked to Hickson, the £251,000 deposited in five banks and eight building societies by John Knight, and the £150,000 deposited at Barclay's Bank in Harrow by Jimmy Knight. In fact, the trial was awash with cash.

Despite valiant efforts by defence counsels to explain this affluence away, John Knight and Terry Perkins were found guilty and sentenced to twenty-two years' imprisonment. Jimmy Knight and Billy Hickson were found not guilty of robbery but guilty of handling stolen money, and sentenced to eight and six years respectively. John Horsley pleaded guilty and was sentenced to eight years. Robert Young, an accountant, was found not guilty of assisting in the disposal of stolen cash. Taken altogether, the gang were sentenced to a total of sixty-six years. Alan Opiola, the supergrass, served three years in protective custody.

DCI Peter Wilton and his Flying Squad team were obviously cock-a-hoop with the convictions and sentences. This particular investigative team were nicknamed the 'Dirty Dozen', as demonstrated by the way they had arrested and charged Diana Knight and her son with perverting the course of justice. These charges were later dismissed by the CPS as having no substance, but this did not prevent Diana from enduring the traumas of a nervous breakdown and divorce. Now that the Dirty Dozen had tasted the sweet blood of victory, they wanted to go after the robbers who still allegedly remained beyond the reach of British law, in Spain.

The principal players on their hit list were Ronnie Knight, Freddie Foreman, a.k.a. the infamous 'Brown Bread Fred', Ronnie Everett, John Mason and Clifford Saxe. Once the UK press and local media heard that British detectives were on the Costa del Sol, investigating the sun-loving cockneys, they embarked on a protracted and intense propaganda campaign, labelling the ex-pats as the 'Famous Five', 'Costa Crooks' and 'Robbers of the Century'.

It was not long before the Spanish authorities commenced extradition proceedings, asking each of them to attend the local Malaga police station, where they had to prove to the authorities the source of their income and that they were not working illegally. Ronnie Knight claimed he had no outstanding matters in Britain, and that he had sold two bars in London. Foreman said that he had income from two businesses in Britain, profits from an American drink distribution company and was investing in property on the Costa del Sol. Everett declared that he had retired, sold his pub in London for £300,000 and was living on the proceeds. Mason said he'd sold his house for £90,000 and had businesses in London. Due to poor health, Saxe was unable to attend the meeting.

In short, the British police were stymied, the 'Famous Five' were long-term, well-behaved, middle-aged residents in Spain and, short of wrapping them up and chucking them on a plane, the Costa del Sol would remain their home.

That was until a new Anglo-Spanish extradition treaty was signed in July 1985, closing a loophole that had existed since 1978. The treaty was not, however, retrospective, so the Famous Five were safe for a while (until mid-July 1989, when the treaty was updated and the Spanish government could expel unwanted residents).

Unfortunately for Freddie Foreman, he had entered the country on a false passport and thus came under the terms of the new extradition policy. On the morning of Friday 28th July 1989, Foreman was leaving his apartment at the El Alcazaba luxury complex in Puerto Banus, Marbella, when he was accosted by Guardia Civil detectives in the car park. He was bundled in a police car and taken to the local nick. This had happened many times before, and he thought that once he'd spoken to his Spanish solicitor he'd sort out the mess and be released.

But at the police station he was not allowed to see his brief. Agitated, he was dragged and bundled into another police vehicle and driven straight to Malaga airport, sedated and flown back to Heathrow, where the Flying Squad were waiting for him. Still in his summer shorts, t-shirt and sandals, Foreman had been drugged, kidnapped and booted out of a country where he had committed no crimes. In next to no time, he was arrested and charged with the Security Express depot robbery, handling stolen money and using a false passport. Whisked away to the magistrate's court, he was remanded in custody to his old *alma mater*, Brixton Prison.

Against his will, he swapped the sun-blessed beaches of Spain for the cold, friendless walls of a prison cell. Never one to mope, Foreman employed the eloquent legal services of John Matthews QC and prepared for battle. Before the trial the police propaganda machine had been well oiled, and the media were digging up all the dirt on Foreman's past links with the Krays and the Great Train Robbers. The prosecution wanted a twenty four-hour guard around the jury, and got it. The Flying Squad made sure the jury witnessed the heavily armed police presence around the Old Bailey. The jurors knew it could only be for one man – Freddie Foreman, the cockney armed robber in court one.

His Honour Judge Stephen Mitchell QC was presiding, and the prosecutor was Michael Worsley QC, now a Security Express veteran. At the heart of the prosecution's case was an alleged confession that Foreman had made to a senior Spanish police officer, the sudden accumulation of wealth, and provable association with other suspected Security Express robbers. The alleged confession was backed by Captain Domingo de Guzman, who claimed that he interviewed Foreman in a Marbella hotel in November 1988. When asked why he was in Spain, Foreman allegedly replied that he had taken part in the Security Express robbery back in England. Surprisingly, however, Foreman's lawyer, Mrs Susan Fernandez, was present at the interview and never heard him confess to any crime.

The second feature of the prosecution case was that Foreman was almost penniless in the months leading up to the robbery. It was alleged that he was living in a council flat, had only £72 in his bank account, and Southwark borough council had lowered his rent from £32 to £7 per week. But after the robbery he had paid more than £360,000 into the Allied Irish Bank at Lewisham and transferred £300,000 to a bank in Marbella. The defence said the bank account with £72 was defunct, and that there was no proof that the £360,000 was money stolen during the Security Express raid.

The jury thought otherwise and found Foreman guilty of

handling stolen money, but not guilty of robbery. He was sentenced – harshly, in my view – to nine years' imprisonment. (The following day he landed at Full Sutton prison, where I met him on the sports field. Just as I was about to get to know the legendary Freddie Foreman there was a riot on my wing, and I was booted out of the jail.)

Not happy with the conviction and sentence of Foreman, the Flying Squad's 'Dirty Dozen' nicked his wife, Maureen, for handling stolen money and let her suffer for a year before the CPS finally said that there was no case to answer. That kind of vindictiveness is the last thing you need while you are serving a long prison sentence.

Meanwhile, back on the Costa del Sol, the extraordinary abduction and extradition of Foreman sent shockwaves throughout the ex-pat community. Who was next, they wondered? The 'Famous Five', now reduced to four, wondered whether to voluntarily return home and face the inevitable, or whether to hang it out until the last minute.

Top of the list was Ronnie Knight. He may not have been the most dangerous fugitive on the Costa del Sol, but he was the most newsworthy. Once married to the cockney actress Barbara Windsor, the rapacious tabloid press had demonised Knight, making him into a larger-than-life figure living it up in Spain, while his two brothers were paying their dues in a British prison. Any incident or event was blown way out of proportion. Removing someone from his bar was exaggerated into a gangland fight; his wedding to his girlfriend, Sue Haylock, was transformed into a media circus with motor launches and helicopters buzzing around his Fuengirola hillside villa. This was further exacerbated when John Knight appealed against the severity of his twenty two-year prison sentence. The Law Lords proclaimed, "If there was such a thing as the mafia in this country, then the Knights were it," and the appeal was refused.

The constant media attention reached such a crescendo that Ronnie seriously thought about returning home and clearing his name. Even Peter Wilton, head of the enquiry, had flown out to Marbella to encourage him to return. The crunch came when a tabloid newspaper and TV company put forward a deal to bring him home. They offered him £45,000 to return and he accepted. When the Lear jet touched down at Luton Airport, Knight was asked if he had anything to declare. "Only my innocence," he replied. The Flying Squad proclaimed that no deal was done for his return. On 3rd May 1994, after nearly eleven years in voluntary exile, Ronnie Knight appeared at Bow Street Magistrate's Court in London and bail was refused. While awaiting trial in Brixton Prison, he reapplied for bail at the Magistrate's Court, the High Court and the Old Bailey – and it was constantly refused, on account of the Dirty Dozen claiming a witness had received threatening telephone calls. Ronnie Knight was in for the long haul.

At the trial, His Honour Judge Gerald Gordon QC presided, Michael Worsley QC was prosecuting again and Richard Ferguson QC was defending. The case against

Knight was to follow the same winning formula as the previous trials. Ronald Knight had fled Britain twenty-four hours after his brother, John, had been arrested for the robbery. He had deposited £314,000 of stolen money with his ex-wife's accountants, Fox Associates (without her knowledge), and transferred some of this to a Spanish bank, to be invested in property. The police also wanted to speak to his new girlfriend, who had allegedly deposited £32,000 in a bank account in Hendon, north London. At the court hearing, Knight offered to plead guilty to handling stolen money in return for the robbery count being dropped. After consultation at the highest level of the Crown Prosecution Service, the Crown was prepared to accept the plea.

During sentencing the judge observed that, although Knight was not an actual robber himself, he had been "very deeply involved". Ronnie Knight later stated that he was expecting five years, but instead he was sentenced to seven years' imprisonment. While in prison, Knight had lots of time to think about the past. While piecing together all the events of the previous few years, he began to suspect that there had been more than one mole in the Security Express depot robbery, with another working for the police.

Some time later, after John Knight was released from his swingeing prison sentence in 1995, he acknowledged that the robbers had their own mystery man on the inside. During several clandestine meetings, the mole had told him about the internal layout of the depot, the control rooms, the cameras in the yard and their weak spots, how the guards washed their cars in the yard, how the solitary guard collected the milk from the hatch, personal details about the employees and, most importantly, how the guards were instructed not to resist during a raid. In essence, Knight was told anything he wanted to know about the depot and its employees. For all this invaluable information, the mole was reputedly paid £10,000.

The Final Analysis

At the time of the Security Express depot job, in 1983, it was classified as the largest cash robbery in British criminal history. A successful team of armed robbers had penetrated and overcome human, physical, and state-of-the-art electronic barriers to steal almost £6 million in untraceable used banknotes. The raid had taken over a year to prepare, and concluded with the robbers waiting the last four hours for the custodians to arrive to unlock the vault. They loaded their getaway vehicles with four tons of cash and simply disappeared into thin air.

A successful robbery may be signified by a paucity of potential leads for the investigation team. In this case there were none. There were no facial identifications, fingerprints, CCTV footage or abandoned vehicles. The only piece of circumstantial evidence was hypothetical, a detective's hunch that there must have been an inside man.

So where did the robbers go wrong? The first major flaw in this crime occurred soon after the robbery, when John Knight, Terry Perkins and Billy Hickson began to involve individuals from the motor trade in their clean-up operation. Whether they were friends of the family or not, it was sheer suicidal laziness to let Alan Opiola and John Horsley have anything to do with the robbery.

Speaking from experience, those in the car trade consistently shed their allegiances to anything or anyone once they are in a police station. As the great German extortionist and ransom taker Arno Funke once explained to me, when speaking about crime and criminals: "One person knows, nobody knows. Two people know, everybody knows."

The second critical flaw was that, because the police had no concrete leads in the case, they were reduced to relying upon information from informers and surveillance of potential suspects. In the time it took the enquiry team to come up to pace with the robbers, it had lulled them into a false sense of security. Being, *inter alia*, successful businessmen, they wanted to put the money to work. In their view, it made little sense to leave it buried in a hole or hidden in a safe deposit box. It was better in a bank or building society accruing interest. The major problem was that, as the robbers became full-fledged targets, they left behind an indelible paper trail of bulging bank accounts across Britain and Europe. The police were no longer interested in evidence found at the scene of the crime; all that mattered was the apparent phoenix-like rise from financial instability to sun-blessed affluence. It was enough evidence to convict.

The police and judiciary are inclined to crow at every opportunity about how crime does not pay. For some, like those who received very long prison sentences for the robbery and handling the stolen money, it patently does not. But for others, like the rest of the gang who went on to enjoy the proceeds of the crime, it obviously does pay. This includes the ever-elusive, mysterious mole who instigated the idea to rob the cash depot from the very outset.

THE KNIGHTSBRIDGE SAFE DEPOSIT CENTRE ROBBERY

12 JULY 1987

On a warm and sunny Sunday afternoon in mid-July 1987, two well-dressed, middle-aged robbers posing as businessmen calmly walked into the Knightsbridge Safe Deposit Centre on Brompton Road, Knightsbridge, central London, overpowered the security staff and walked out with an estimated £20-£60 million in cash, priceless jewellery and pure, uncut cocaine. Within a matter of days, Scotland Yard had an all-important lead: the man they wanted to question about what was dubbed 'the robbery of the century' was an Italian master villain called Valerio Viccei. This is his story, the tale of how one man overcame the most secure safe deposit centre in the world.

Valerio 'Gigi' Viccei was born in the picturesque town of Ascoli Piceno, near the Adriatic coast of Italy. His father was a well-respected libel lawyer and his mother ran a successful boutique, which she inherited from her own mother. Along with his younger brother and sister, he had a bright and vibrant future ahead of him. In Gigi's autobiography, he claims that he never wanted for anything as a child. Money was never short, and there was always plenty of good food on the table. If he wanted toys, he had them. If he wanted the best clothes, he had them. Through his parents' hard work and diligence, the Vicceis enjoyed a comfortable home and lifestyle.

Not much is known about Gigi's school years, whether or not he was academically minded or preferred sport. He admits, however, to having a bad temper, and would feel frustrated if things were not going his way. In many ways, having a fiery disposition should not be misconstrued as a negative trait, as passion and drive invariably come from rawness of character.

We do know that Gigi obtained a grammar school leaving certificate and enrolled at a local university to study law. It was here that he was introduced to the discipline of philosophy, which helped to shape his outlook on life. He had a particular admiration for the German poet-philosopher Friedrich Nietzsche, noted for his concept of 'the superman' and his rejection of traditional Christian values. Some evidence of this can be seen in his teens, when Gigi began to thrive on the personal realisation that, as a person, he was becoming stronger, and anything was now possible. He claims that he developed a predatory instinct bolstered by his innate love of the opposite sex and lethal firearms. In essence, Gigi had become highly individualistic, and craved a high-risk, sensation-seeking lifestyle. This is echoed in one of his favourite Nietzschean aphorisms: "For believe me – the secret of realising the greatest fruitfulness and greatest enjoyment of existence is to live dangerously."

He was completely disillusioned with studying law at university, and soon found himself embroiled in the increasingly murky world of extremist politics. It is alleged that he joined the rightwing youth group *Fronta Della Giuventu*, and became an ardent activist, volunteering for the most dangerous of missions. Gigi was not one to daub swastikas on public buildings and walls; he was a passionate idealist who wanted to be at the centre of the action.

In 1972, at the relatively tender age of seventeen, he had already participated in the planting of explosives and the bombing of a major national TV station. As he wanted to strike at bigger, more prestigious targets, it has been alleged that Gigi attempted to blow up the Milan to Lecce Trans-Europe Express train, carrying fifteen hundred passengers, and, even more extreme perhaps, to blow up a dam at Lake Compotosto, which would have caused widespread flooding and destruction of villages along the Adriatic coastline.

What is obvious is that life was too boring for Gigi; he could not endure a mundane existence. He had transformed from an adolescent rascal with a craving for adventure and firearms into a well-organised terrorist.

Central to his school of thought was that he could not abide the rules and values that Italian society was trying to foist upon him. In many respects, his path into dark criminality was already set.

It is believed that his first armed robberies were committed in order to finance his terrorist activities. Whatever the case, he claims to have committed his first serious blag at the age of nineteen. It was not long before he had come to the attention of the police, and was arrested for trying to obtain a firearm while using a forged licence. His arrest and subsequent six-month imprisonment were, he claimed, due to a police informer. To some degree, his sentence served as a warning that there was a heavy price to pay for committing serious crimes. But prison can be an education, and he was determined to learn from it.

By the age of twenty-one, Gigi had become the smartest villain in the region, with a taste for snazzy suits and expensive jewellery, luxurious cars, posh hotels and restaurants. He adored women, and had his eye on a girl named Neomi who lived in a nearby village. Her vigilant parents were dead against the two of them coming together, but the Viccei charm and charisma knew no bounds and they soon became one in marriage.

By now, Gigi had a string of armed bank robberies under his belt, and his healthy contempt for the law only compounded his booming confidence. Gigi was not a cash-in-transit robber, intercepting the money as it was delivered across the pavement to banks and other financial institutions. He was a very bold over-the-counter man. His forte was to enter a bank wearing a facial disguise, secure the public area with his favourite semiautomatic Beretta pistol, leap over the cashier's counter and rifle the tills and safe.

Evidently, Gigi and his gang were so proficient at this storming technique that the banks were wont to leave a trap for them. They planted something called a 'bait bundle' of recognisable banknotes in the strong-room or safe. These specific notes were photographed and had all their serial numbers logged. Should the bank be robbed and the perpetrators apprehended with the planted proceeds at a later date, this compelling evidence could naturally lead to a conviction. But Gigi was aware of the ruse, as a bent copper on his payroll had forewarned him.

Gigi and his gang robbed another bank outside of the region and, knowing what to look for, took the bait bundle from the safe, recognisable by the green elastic bands that held it together. He decided to dispose of the money quickly by paying off an outstanding drug debt. But, unbeknownst to Gigi, a gang member would return some drugs as they were of poor quality. The dealer paid him with banknotes from the bundle, and, within a short space of time, the stolen money had travelled full circle and was back in Gigi's possession.

Subsequently, when the local robbery squad called at Gigi and Neomi's place, they found banknotes that matched serial numbers on their bait bundle list. Gigi was carted off to the main police station and charged with bank robbery. Things looked grim.

To aggravate matters, he and other gang members were implicated in a litany of robberies by a supergrass. Gigi was found guilty and sentenced to eleven years' imprisonment. With another grass waiting in the wings to give incriminating evidence, he decided a change of tactics was necessary. Rightly or wrongly, he decided to subvert the supergrass's evidence by pleading guilty to innumerable bank robberies – even to some that he had been acquitted of in the past – and giving up a large cache of firearms that were buried in the Ascoli area.

In the mysterious ways of the Italian justice system, however, the cumulative effect of a full confession and the surrendering of the hidden firearms allowed him to be released on bail pending appeal. (At that time he still had another eight years' imprisonment to serve.)

While in prison he had received loving visits from his wife Neomi, who provided him with all the necessities that a long-term prisoner would require. Over the course of time, nonetheless, the regular visits began to wane and he noticed an appreciable change in her appearance and attitude. The sparkle in her eye had died. He sensed the change was because she had started to hang out with lowlife drug addicts, and others who circulated rumours that Gigi had had other lovers while they were married. The playboy image had returned to haunt him. Now, he believed, it was he who was being cuckolded.

But as Gigi painfully describes, worse was to come. While he was in prison, he later claimed, Neomi had metamorphosed into a full-fledged drug addict and police informant. Released on bail, pending appeal, he was planning another bank robbery outside his bail zone. Gigi, Neomi and another accomplice were returning from a reconnaissance mission in the countryside when they came to a motorway toll booth. Sensing danger, Gigi told the driver to stop well before the booth, which enabled him to assess the surrounding area for police activity. Gigi was just about to give the order to continue when he spotted two distinctive car aerials on a concealed police car beyond some bushes. He told his anxious accomplice to take off sharply, and that is when the police activity on the radio scanner in his vehicle burst into life. It was a 'ready eye', a pre-planned trap where armed police with loaded machineguns were lying in wait for him.

Gigi sensed that this was more than a routine covert surveillance operation, and that someone was supplying them with specific information. It was not long before the spotlight of suspicion fell upon his now estranged wife, Neomi. It did not take Gigi long to realise that, though his stringent bail conditions had been revoked, he would still have to face another eight years in the shovel. His wife was a 'wrong 'un', and, as anyone with a modicum of commonsense should have recognised, when you are in a hole you stop digging.

Sometime in late December 1985, Gigi decided it was

time to flee his native land. Armed with a false passport, a suitcase and a significant amount of cash, he caught a high-speed international train to Switzerland and then another train to Paris. His destination was England. As soon as he left Italy and successfully passed through several frontier checkpoints he felt an overwhelming sense of relief and tranquillity. (Regrettably, however, he had to dump his favourite Walther pistol.) As he arrived in Paris, he was on the cusp of seeing out the old year. In a matter of minutes it would be 1986; the dawn of a promising new era for him.

After downing a few French beers, he rang his mother and remained on the phone for as long as he dared. Afterwards, he vowed to himself that he would never give up; he would stay free and return to see her once again. In spite of the powerful longing to be back among the comfort of familiar surroundings, he knew that he was in an awkward dilemma. He could either remain in Italy and face many years in the claustrophobic confines of a cold, colourless prison, or become a fun-loving fugitive in a world that was new to him.

There was not much choice. There was no way that he was going to volunteer for another dire spell in prison. Cold logic dictated that life on the run was far more dynamic and adventurous. Who knew what fortuitous breaks and opportunities would arise in a beautiful city like London? He took a long, deep breath, and felt better already.

The next morning he caught the first available ferry to

Dover, and then a train to Victoria station. His initial impression of the capital was not good. He could hardly speak a word of English, did not know how to work a public telephone, and desperately needed to contact an old Italian friend who had set up camp with his English girlfriend in the city. He cursed the strange language, the telephone system and the wretched weather. But he still had hope.

Later that day, Gigi managed to contact his Italian compatriot and arranged to stay at his address. It soon dawned on him that his welcome was not as warm as it ought to have been, and he decided to seek alternative accommodation. Through his Italian friend he managed to secure a central London flat, where he would also seduce the gorgeous Swedish landlady. During the several weeks he spent with her, their time was mostly spent in bed. But Gigi knew that his financial resources would not last forever. He had to obtain some firearms, find a bank to rob and steal a motorbike for the rapid getaway.

Spotting a motorbike in Berkeley Square, he surveyed the area, pushed it around the corner, busted the ignition and steering lock, and roared away through Park Lane. It was not long, however, before he was rigorously pursued by a succession of marked police vehicles, with their blue lights flashing and sirens blaring. Gigi knew from experience that stealing motorbikes very rarely came on top this quickly, so he powered away and dumped the machine in a secluded alleyway.

When he met up with his Italian partner later to discuss the strange sequence of events, he was told that it was a legal necessity in Britain to wear a crash helmet, and that is why he was chased by the police. Cursing his friend and his luck, he fared better in obtaining the tools for the job. After numerous meets and cancellations with some guys in Hatton Garden, he managed to obtain a semiautomatic Beretta pistol and a decrepit old single-barrel shotgun with ammunition. He stole another motorbike and, in the spring of 1986, decided to rob a branch of the prestigious Coutts Bank in Sloane Avenue – otherwise known as 'the Queen's bank'. He found this so easy that he decided to rob another branch in Cavendish Square – only this time, while he was behind the cashier's counter, raking in the cash, the hydraulic, stainless steel anti-bandit panel shot up and blocked his exit. Not one to panic in a crisis, Gigi kept his cool and made one of the female cashiers retract the anti-bandit screen to enable him and his accomplice to escape.

All in all, Gigi successfully robbed five banks in central London. These included a small branch of the Midland Bank in Curzon Street, Mayfair. Although there are no precise figures of the sums stolen in these robberies, it is estimated that Gigi and his bold accomplice escaped with anything up to £500,000. Most of this money was needed to pay for the exorbitant rents charged by landlords in central London, and to maintain Gigi's lavish image as a playboy serial seducer among the chic Mayfair set.

For no matter what we think about Gigi, he definitely

had style. He rented a luxurious flat in the posh area of St John's Wood, northwest London. He treated himself to a top-of the range Ferrari Mondial; wore the finest Armani suits, gold watches and handmade suede and leather shoes; ate at all the best restaurants in London, and shared a passion for sipping pink champagne and snorting the purest cocaine with his peers. Some would say that he was an ultra-flash, arrogant and vain thug. I would say that this man knew the unique value of money, and exactly how to enjoy it. As he later proclaimed, "If you have the money there's no point looking at it in the bank collecting dust, you may as well appreciate it."

(Coincidentally, at the same time Gigi was living a playboy fugitive existence in the capital, so, to a lesser degree, was I. In November 1984 I had escaped from prison, having only served two years of a fifteen-year sentence for armed robbery. I was advised by close friends that the best place to lie low was in central London, as its multicultural and cosmopolitan mixture of people made it the perfect place to become anonymous. Admittedly, whereas Gigi hobnobbed it with the affluent Mayfair set and surrounded himself with the luxuries of Ferrari, Rolex, Armani and Louis Vuitton, I was firmly ensconced amongst the Sloanies in Chelsea, sporting the latest BMW and, a little less conspicuously, Cartier, Cecil Gee and Gucci. We were unlikely to bump into each other either socially or when we were both working. But until I was rearrested, in June 1986, we were both living the same nervous-yet-exhilarating existence, dreading the day when by sheer chance we would be apprehended and thrown back into the dark world of long-term imprisonment. It is from this unique position that I can empathise with Gigi's precarious predicament. He already had one foot in a prison cell, and in a sense it gave him a licence to plunder the banks of London for all that they were worth. The feeling and the experience were mutual.)

Not surprisingly, the image of the Ferrari-loving playboy nearly led to Gigi's undoing. On one cold January morning in 1987, he was leaving his luxury flat in St John's Wood when his animal instincts forewarned him of an unusual amount of strange activity. As he warmed the engine of his white Ferrari Mondial – registered in the name of a close friend, Israel Pinkas – he noticed an unmarked police car going past and decided he would drive away from the area. He got as far as St John's Wood Road, at the junction with Wellington Road, when he was boxed in by police vehicles. He slipped his brain out of neutral and decided to play the role of the surprised and aggrieved foreign driver, caught up in a confusing incident.

But as he sat in the passenger seat of a stationary police car, he was told the police had received information that he was a suspected fugitive on the run from Italy, and that there was a warrant for his arrest and extradition. It was also suggested that the police should take no chances with him, as the information received suggested that he may well be armed. This was enough for Gigi to realise he could not wait around to be carted off to a decrepit British prison. So he smashed the police sergeant next to him in the face, booted the car door into the groin of the cozzer standing outside and bolted down the road like fear had given wings to his feet. After jumping over a succession of gardens and running through a carwash he managed, against all odds, to make good his escape.

And this is where the remarkable story of Gigi gets very interesting. During the commotion of the police blocking in the Ferrari, several people from nearby shops and businesses came out to observe the unfolding drama. Many of them watched him make his extraordinary escape from the police. Some of the onlookers were from a nearby St John's Wood branch of the Knightsbridge Safe Deposit Centre where, several months previously, Gigi had opened a deposit account. He had the proceeds of several bank robberies concealed in the box, and soon realised he had to retrieve the contents before they told the police they knew the identity of the fleeing suspect.

Gigi decided to send a new female customer – his current squeeze – into the safe deposit centre that afternoon to open an account. She would return later the same evening with his unique swipe card and six-digit pin number, access Gigi's box and retrieve his goods. But the plan failed, as the computerised security system in place recognised that she was not the owner of the box. When accosted by the managing director of the centre, she was told only the owner could have access to it.

Upon hearing about the failed plan, Gigi sensed that there may have been a sting involved. If he did not return to retrieve the contents of his box when the annual contract ran out, the owners could force it open and confiscate the contents. Gigi decided to call the managing director of the safe deposit centre, Parvez Latif, and speak to him personally. In no uncertain terms, he said that if the contents of his box were touched he would hold Latif personally responsible and seek revenge. Latif replied that if Gigi sent someone with power of attorney over his affairs, he could have legitimate access to the box and its contents. Gigi had no option but to fly a close relative over from Italy the next day, to visit his safe deposit box and retrieve its contents.

The remarkable aspect about this episode is the initial contact between Latif and Gigi, vault manager and armed robber. If Gigi had been arrested at the police roadblock, the chances are that they would never have met or spoken to each other again. But this minor episode of conflict would change the direction of both their lives.

Sensing that someone close to him, either in Britain or his native Italy, must have told of his whereabouts, Gigi decided to take a vacation to South America. While he was on holiday he sent the managing director of the safe deposit centre a 'thank you' postcard. At this time, he thought no more about the incident and decided to let the matter fade. On returning to Britain, however, Gigi was having a quiet romantic meal with a blonde girlfriend called Tamara, in an elegant West End restaurant, when she declared that she knew Parvez Latif on a social level and had shared cocaine with him. Immediately, alarm bells started to ring inside Gigi's head. The potent mix of alcohol, cocaine and beautiful women all equated with one thing: an inherent vulnerability that could be exploited. Things were looking up.

The next day, Gigi reached for his Yellow Pages local telephone directory and rang Latif at the sister branch of the safe deposit centre in Knightsbridge, opposite the world-famous Harrods superstore. He spoke to Latif and was invited to meet him at the centre. Gigi knew that he had to make an imposing impression. He wanted to come across as a man of wealth and substance, of culture and class, as someone that could be of use to Latif both on a social and a business level. For Gigi knew from experience that straight people were often intimidated by villainous characters, and did not want to exude the unprepossessing image of a businessman living on the edge of a shady existence. He sensed that a subtle combination of his upper middleclass breeding, style and expensive tastes could pull it off.

On arrival at the rear entrance to the safe deposit centre, Gigi began to survey the area and immediately saw its potential. The semi-suburban sleepiness of Cheval Place radiated a warm glow inside his soul. He liked what he saw. Initially the conversation was tense but, after a guided tour of the vault in the basement, both men settled down to discuss recent events in the office. Gigi thanked Latif profusely for saving him from "unmentionable problems" regarding the St John's Wood affair, and also mentioned a social connection with his current girlfriend, Tamara. Gigi decided not to beat about the bush with incessant smalltalk, and reached into his bag to retrieve a small container with a large rock of pure cocaine inside. Latif's eyes lit up, and they shared a line of charlie together. This was a significant watershed in their relationship. The door was open.

Over the coming weeks Gigi visited the safe deposit centre more than was necessary, to sweet-talk Latif and gain his confidence. More often than not they shared a line of cocaine or two, and it was not before long they were going out socially as a foursome with girlfriends in tow, enjoying the exquisite gastronomic fare that comes with West End decadence. There was only one problem. Latif's current girlfriend, Pamela Seamarks, a gorgeous, leggy blonde with a voluptuous body, made it obvious that she was discontented with her beau. After a while she made it plain that she was up for some action, and it was only a matter of time before Gigi gatecrashed her skimpy knickers. This could obviously put the plan to rob the safe deposit centre in serious jeopardy. As much as he could, he had to tap into some kind of self-discipline.

In the meantime, Gigi wanted to find some much-needed monetary resources to bring Latif into line with the notion that robbing the centre would be a mutually beneficial exercise. Gigi decided to pull off one more robbery and chose the American Express branch in Mount Street, off Park Lane, Mayfair. He entered the building with an accomplice and secured the public area of the bank, vaulted the cashier's screen and escaped with a significant amount of cash and unsigned traveller's cheques.

Later that week, he slipped over to see Latif at the safe deposit centre and asked if he could cash the traveller's cheques for him. Latif did this and was rewarded handsomely for his troubles. It did not take long for Latif to realise what shady profession his new Italian friend was involved in, and to agree to help Gigi rob the most secure safe deposit centre in the world.

For a moment Gigi had to pinch himself, as he could not believe he had the man in control of an Aladdin's cave of riches firmly in his pocket. But it's one thing to talk about such a sizeable robbery, another to plan and successfully achieve it. Gigi knew unreservedly that this was going to be the biggest robbery of his life, but with the support and assistance of an inside man it was achievable.

The first task he set himself was to make a list of how, when and with what manpower and equipment he would commit the robbery. For, as the old adage goes, "If you fail to plan, you plan to fail." He decided that he could pull it off with a total of five men – including him – at the centre, and another waiting at the flop to help him unload the proceeds.

After three months of observations, planning and

organising, he decided the robbery of the century would go ahead on Sunday 12 July 1987. Gigi chose a Sunday as Latif had given him photocopies of the safe deposit centre visitors' logbook, and he knew the quietest time during opening hours at the centre was between 3 to 5pm on a Sunday afternoon.

On the day of the robbery, Gigi and his accomplice went to a public telephone box in nearby Pont Street, Knightsbridge. He rang Latif at the centre, pretending to be a genuine businessman, and asked if it was possible to assess the security arrangements at the centre before deciding whether or not to open a deposit account. Latif agreed to this, and forewarned the two uniformed security guards in the centre – one in the bullet-proof control centre at the rear of the building, one at the front desk – to expect two potential customers. This was normal procedure.

Once inside, they were greeted by Latif and given a guided tour of the complex. Once in the basement vault, Latif showed Gigi and his accomplice the private viewing room where depositors could access their box in private. This had no internal CCTV coverage. Inside the private viewing room, Gigi extracted a handgun and shotgun from his briefcase and explained to Latif that this was a bona fide robbery. With a pistol firmly pressed into his back, they frogmarched Latif over to the bullet-proof control room, where Latif asked the security guard to let him inside so that they could show the customers how effectively the security arrangements worked. Once inside,

Gigi overpowered the guard and chained him to a concrete pillar in the basement. They did the same to the guard stationed at the front desk. Now they had complete control of the centre. Using walkie-talkies, Gigi then ordered another accomplice, wearing a similar uniform to the genuine security guards, to position himself at the front of the centre to deal with any unexpected customers or queries. He also placed a purpose-made placard in both the street-level entrances of the building declaring that the premises were temporarily closed:

> We apologize to all our Customers
> For any inconvenience caused to
> Them during the improvements to
> Our security system.
> Business as usual from tomorrow
> Thank you.

Once this had been achieved, the next stage was to call two other accomplices parked in a large Renault van to fetch all the power tools, sledgehammers, large screwdrivers and crowbars required to break into the boxes and large sacks, and to carry the proceeds away. Frustratingly, Gigi could not get through to them on the walkie-talkie. He checked the pre-programmed frequency of his radio transceiver and all seemed okay. Getting increasingly anxious, he decided to leave the safe confines of the centre and bring the two men himself.

As he stepped outside the rear entrance of the premises, he bumped into a solitary uniformed policeman and calmly said, "Good afternoon" to him. Receiving a similar reply, he looked further down the road and could see more policemen and vehicles. (Later, he learned that a small girl had been reported missing and they were searching for her.) He managed to catch up with his two accomplices, laughing and joking in the Renault van. He checked their walkie-talkies and found that they were on another frequency. Nearly bursting a blood vessel in his rage, he beckoned them to follow him back into the safe deposit centre.

They had entered the centre at 3:00pm. It was now 3:20pm and Gigi wanted to get on with the main part of breaking into the safe deposit boxes. First he ordered Latif to sit inside the bullet-proof control room and answer any incoming calls. Gigi smashed into the largest boxes first, measuring 15 x 15 x 25 inches. The first box was brimming with new £50 and £20 notes, the next replete with new $100 bills, the next Swiss thousand-franc notes, and so on. Busting into the boxes went on and on for the next two hours. There were gold rings, watches and bracelets with precious stones, emeralds and diamonds the size of pigeon eggs, platinum and gold ingots, gold Krugerrands and clocks, high-value paintings, statues, stamps and bonds, even a substantial amount of top-grade cocaine. Anything and everything that was of some monetary value was secreted away in this treasure trove of wealth and excess.

And then of course there were perverse and indecent personal photographs, which could embarrass or compromise members of the aristocracy or the celebrity world, and illegal firearms. As the boxes were being pummelled open and the sacks of luscious loot filled, Gigi had not noticed, in his overriding enthusiasm, that he had torn a gaping hole in his leather gloves and his hand was bleeding. On closer examination, he noticed specks of his blood were everywhere – on the boxes, the tools, carpet, cabinets, and even on the shirts of the security guards, still chained to the concrete pillar in the private viewing room. He bit his lip, as he knew that leaving such powerful evidence behind was a crucial and momentous error.

Thinking on his feet, Gigi thought fleetingly about the idea of burning the whole building down. But that meant leaving the premises to bring the petrol containers, and transporting the security guards and Latif to another location. Because no matter what the media say about Gigi, despite his teenage involvement in terrorism, in the final reckoning he was no cold-blooded killer. He ultimately decided, whether rightly or wrongly, to push on with his original plan and work on smashing open the boxes right up to 5pm – when the third mobile security guard supervisor was due to arrive at the centre, to lock the vault and turn on the alarm system. The supervisor turned up on cue, and was quickly overpowered and chained to the concrete pillar.

Apart from the tragic hole in Gigi's leather glove and the

blood smeared everywhere, and a customer ringing the centre to ask why it was shut, the whole operation was going exactly as planned. Gigi was still energetically breaking into the safe deposit boxes when he was told it was time to go. The five-strong gang began to carry large green sacks up to the ground floor level, ready to be transported via the white Renault getaway van parked outside the rear entrance. In typically headstrong and individualistic fashion, Gigi demanded to drive the van away from the centre. After pulling off one of the most spectacular robberies in British criminal history, he dropped off the gang at prearranged points on the journey to his rented safe-house in Hampstead. For he had insisted on going to the safe-house alone with the loot and, remarkably, the other members of the gang went along with this decision.

From experience, I know that serious professional robbers would not have agreed to this unusual request – no matter what the circumstances – as one of the overriding high points of any successful crime is to share out the proceeds in the presence of all central participants. This meant that Gigi was not only going to take the lion's share, but that the amateur gang he had assembled would be on wages, not an equal cut. In fact, Gigi and Latif were to share a third each of the proceeds and the other third was to be shared out by the other four principal gang members.

At the safe-house in Hampstead, Gigi was met by Stephen Mann, who had rented the third-floor penthouse and acquired a lock-up garage nearby. Jointly they transferred twelve large sacks of loot from the van to the lock-up garage, where they put the proceeds into three large wooden trunks. They dumped the van nearby and came back with a VW Passat estate car. One trunk at a time, they put them inside the estate vehicle and ferried them to the penthouse. Later, Gigi openly admitted that, if he did not have anyone else there to help him, he would not have been able to carry the heavy trunks up the stairs to the penthouse.

Once all the trunks were firmly ensconced in the penthouse, he fulfilled a secret fantasy and filled the bathtub with banknotes. Physically and mentally exhausted, he took a shower and sipped from an ice-cold bottle of Krug champagne before drifting off into a long, deep sleep. It had been a long and laborious day, perhaps the hardest and most rewarding day's work he had ever done. But it would prove costly.

He awoke early in the morning, as brilliant sunshine was beaming through the large bay windows in the front room. He could not focus his eyes, as the sun was refracting up from the countless diamonds, sapphires and emeralds that were strewn around the floor. It was so bright that he had to wear sunglasses to protect his optic nerves. He wanted to watch the national TV news to see what the media were saying about the raid, but first had to sort out the loot and pay the rest of the gang their £100,000 wages.

It was another twenty-four hours before news of the robbery was broadcast by the media. National newspapers and TV news programmes ran the story that the most secure safe deposit centre in the world – with two-foot thick walls, armed security guards, bullet-proof glass, infrared and sound detectors – had been overcome by two well-dressed robbers posing as businessmen.

As the scene-of-crime specialists sifted through the ransacked boxes looking for evidence, the safe deposit centre was besieged by anxious depositors desperate to find out if their property had been stolen. As they queued up outside the centre to be interviewed, passing motorists and taxi drivers could be heard shouting, with a tinge of *Schadenfreude*, "It couldn't have happened to a better bunch of people!" It appeared there was some public support for the pseudo-gentlemanly robbers.

Scotland Yard detectives announced that it would be almost impossible to compile a complete or accurate inventory of cash and property stolen, as many depositors – including wealthy American, European and Middle Eastern millionaires, gold and diamond dealers, royalty, celebrities and known criminals – would not want to reveal exactly what riches and contraband they had in their boxes, for fear of being pursued by the police, customs, Inland Revenue, or various other law enforcement agencies around the world. There were allegedly four thousand safe deposit boxes stored at the centre, of various sizes. Only the largest were rifled, and, most significantly, only eighty of the one hundred and forty-seven box owners came forward to report their losses.

Initial conservative estimates put the haul at £9-10 million, but this soon shot up to £20-£60 million. Scotland Yard announced that they were looking for a small team of robbers described as "audacious and skilful". *The Guardian* published a photofit of one of the robbers, describing him as approximately thirty to forty years old, of Mediterranean appearance and speaking with a Spanish or Italian accent.

It transpires that the police were working in the sweltering safe deposit vault for eight days. It is rumoured that, after three days, they found a perfect bloodstained fingerprint and matched it to Valerio 'Gigi' Viccei, who had absconded from an eight-year prison sentence in Italy and was wanted by the Italian authorities for questioning about fifty-four outstanding armed robberies. Several months before the Knightsbridge robbery, the Italians had alerted Interpol, who sent his personal details and a complete set of his fingerprints to police forces all over Europe.

Meanwhile, in spite of being the most wanted man on earth, Gigi used various aliases to jet around the world with the delectable Pamela Seamarks, selling the stolen gemstones to the highest bidder. Evidently he visited Belgium, Israel and Latin America, opening numbered bank accounts at all these locations. Far from keeping a low profile, he was the living embodiment of the international jet-setting playboy super-villain. His thirst for the fast life of champagne, caviar, cocaine and sex could not be slaked. His overwhelming confidence and contempt for his safety was bordering on the insane. In fact, he would later allude to himself as a "romantic lunatic". Remarkably, less than a month after the raid, he was driving around Mayfair in his brand new £87,000 black Ferrari Testarossa, staying at White's hotel in Bayswater, and wining and dining at his favourite restaurants and nightclubs. This devil-may-care master criminal was behaving like an unalloyed amateur.

On 12 August 1987, almost a month after the robbery, covert police surveillance teams under an operation codenamed Crest had many of Gigi's known associates under constant observation. One of them was Israel Pinkas, the Israeli whose name Gigi had used to register his white Ferrari Mondial when he escaped from the police at St John's Wood, back in January. The surveillance team saw Pinkas enter White's hotel and, after a while, witnessed Gigi leave in his black Ferrari. Detectives followed the Ferrari to Marble Arch in unmarked police vehicles, boxed it in and arrested him. In the back of the Ferrari police recovered over £2 million in diamonds, cash and bank slips which were traceable to accounts all over Europe. It was rumoured that Gigi had returned to Britain from Latin America so that he could ship his beloved Ferrari out of the country.

He was taken to the nearby, top-security Paddington Green police station, where he made a full and frank confession to the crime. During his stay at the station he composed a statement written in Italian and addressed to 'the Magistrate'. In it he calls the robbery "an unrepeatable adventure", and claims that he was "always waiting to reach something that was the top of its field". More altruistically, he insisted, "I have not dragged anyone in the mud, neither have I tried to avoid my responsibilities; if I could be the only one to pay and see all the others free, I would not care the price." It appears that, even in the police station, he had to be the unrestrained extrovert and steal the spotlight. Not only had he made what was already the most professional police force in the world look embarrassingly good, he was doing their job for them by wantonly bragging about how well he carried out the crime.

Almost simultaneously, armed police raided other addresses all over London and arrested a whole gaggle of characters from various nationalities and backgrounds, speaking various mother tongues. Some of them – including David Poole, Eric Rubin and Helle Skovbon – maintained their honour and dignity, refusing to suffer the 'let me help you' nonsense of their interrogators. Others – such as the inside man Parvez Latif, Peter O'Donohue, Israel Pinkas, Stephen Mann and Pamela Seamarks – were like rats on a sinking ship, scrabbling over each other to save themselves. For the man leading the investigation, Detective Inspector Dick Leach, and his team, it was probably the easiest major crime in British criminal history to solve. They were cock-a-hoop, as they had also recovered £5 million of the haul, some of it from other safe deposit boxes.

After being charged with the crime of the century, Gigi and his gang appeared at Horseferry Road Magistrate's Court and were remanded in custody to face trial. At Brixton Prison, Gigi was allocated to a small High Secure Unit called 'A' Segregation. Here he met a wide variety of colourful armed robbers and villains awaiting trial, some of whom he became very good friends with. (Unfortunately, decorum forbids me to mention them by name.) Gigi was like the best-looking bird at a party; everyone wanted a piece of him. He was exciting, charming, a thoroughbred extrovert.

Ironically, now that Gigi was amongst some of the best villains in the capital, he did not want to sit about and let the slowly methodical wheels of justice take their course. He wanted out. Plans were afoot to smuggle a handgun into the unit, and a substantial amount of money was paid for the tool, but he was ripped off. Henceforth, Gigi would be extremely circumspect about any internal offers of help and assistance.

Around about the time that Gigi was in Britain, a veteran armed robber had fled to Spain after a series of raids. While he was in Spain he asked an old criminal friend – a super-rich drug baron – for a loan of £20,000 to prolong his sojourn. But the drug baron was wary of the fugitive's own drug habits, and refused to help him. The fugitive robber returned to Britain and was eventually arrested, and remanded to the same HSU as Gigi.

When the Knightsbridge Safe Deposit Centre robbery went down, the drug baron in Spain reputedly lost nearly £1 million from his deposit box at the centre. So he wanted his money back. He asked about, and found out that the needy fugitive who he refused to help some months earlier was incarcerated with Gigi. He sent a message to the former friend, asking him to slip into Gigi and order him to return the money – or else. But the armed robber, remembering the painful knockback he received from his so-called friend in Spain, refused to do it. So the overriding moral of this tale is, "Think first before refusing to help a friend, as you never know when you might need a favour."

In December 1988, some eighteen months after their arrests, Gigi and his gang went on trial for the Knightsbridge Safe Deposit Centre robbery at the Old Bailey. In spite of making a protracted written confession statement in Italian, Gigi pleaded not guilty, and put forward the defence that this was not an armed robbery at all, as they had permission from their inside man, Latif, to burgle the centre. The defence case was that this was not robbery, but a glorified form of theft.

The defence was seriously undermined, however, on two distinct levels. Firstly, the definition of robbery is that the person under attack is in fear for his or her life. In Gigi's case, the fact that three security guards feared the use of firearms made it tantamount to robbery. The second crucial factor was Stephen Mann, the person who provided the safe-house in Hampstead and helped Gigi unload the stolen proceeds from the getaway van – and who also turned grass and gave evidence for the Crown.

In any event, this did not dampen Gigi's irrepressible charm and charisma. He was forever playing the clown in court, even to the extent of wearing a T-shirt with the slogan, 'Why Me!' On 30 January 1989, after a forty-six-day trial, the jury returned with unanimous guilty verdicts. During sentencing, Judge Lymbery QC opined, "The raid was beyond the ordinary run of armed robberies," being "meticulously planned and executed". He added that, "if you play the game for colossal stakes" and lose, then the consequences are dire.

The judge sentenced Gigi to twenty-two years' imprisonment for the Knightsbridge Safe Deposit Centre robbery and, after he pleaded guilty to five armed robberies in central London between April 1986 to May 1987, to another seventeen years to run concurrently. He also sentenced Parvez Latif to eighteen years, David Poole to sixteen years, Eric Rubin to twelve years, Peter O'Donohue to eleven years and Israel Pinkas to ten years, cut to nine on appeal. Pamela Seamarks and Helle Skovbon pleaded guilty to receiving stolen goods and received suspended prison sentences, making one hundred and five years in total.

Due to his perceived dangerousness, his access to considerable wealth and his very long prison sentence, Gigi was classified as a triple-A category prisoner, the highest security classification in British prisons. He was allocated to the Special Secure Unit (SSU) at Parkhurst Prison on the Isle of Wight, where I briefly had the chance to meet him as we were being escorted to the high-risk visiting room at the jail. He cut a rather dapper and imperious figure, like a self-admiring Napoleon, as the four screws and the dog handler chaperoned him to the changing room. We acknowledged each other and went on our separate ways.

During his time in the SSU, he attended educational classes to improve his English and penned his autobiography, *Knightsbridge: The Robbery of the Century*. He also regularly corresponded with his previous girlfriends and the senior detective who arrested him, the now promoted Detective Chief Inspector Leach. Over time they reputedly forged a friendship out of mutual respect for each other. This led to the detective recovering some of the Knightsbridge spoils over and above those that were already seized, information about gangland executions and the supposed truth about Roberto Calvi, 'God's Banker', who was found hanged under Blackfriars Bridge in 1982.

The mutual friendship must have paid dividends. Along with support from Judge Lymbery QC, and overtures made to the Home Office by his former socialite friend's husband, Tory MP Sir Anthony Buck, in November 1992 he was extradited under the Treaty of Strasbourg to serve the remainder of his sentence in an Italian prison.

Later, in a tabloid newspaper, DCI Leach advised all rookie cops to take note of his friendship with Viccei, stressing how, in order "to get information you have to engage with people". After he was extradited, Leach visited Gigi in Italy.

After serving five years of a swingeing twenty-two-year prison sentence, the man who masterminded the Knightsbridge raid swapped a cell at Parkhurst for another one at Pescara, along the Adriatic coast. The only distinction was that this was a prison for the *pentiti*, Mafia supergrasses who collaborated with the Italian judicial system in exchange for fast-tracked freedom and privileges.

Gigi was allowed out during the day to work at a publisher's office, returning every night by 10:30pm. He quickly rented a love-pad in the seaside town and made up for lost time by bedding a succession of beautiful women. As he later told a British journalist, "I was not sentenced to chastity." Gigi was back. He was due for a parole review in 2003 and, being a reformed and "exemplary prisoner", it looked like a mere formality.

But maybe the money had run dry, the financial road to freedom proven too costly, or else he simply longed for the forbidden excitement of committing dangerous crimes. For Gigi had returned to his old ways. On 18 April 2000, he was travelling in a stolen Lancia Thema with two other men, along a country road in the Abruzzi province of Teramo, one hundred miles east of Rome, a remote road used by prostitutes. One of the other men was a well-known *pentiti* called Antonio Malatesta, a member of the Puglia Mafia (known as 'the Sacred Heart').

A routine traffic patrol saw three men in the vehicle and thought them suspicious. The two officers pulled the car over and approached the vehicle with machineguns drawn. As the short, sharp seconds raced by, Gigi knew that this was not good. He pulled out his .357 Magnum and blasted traffic cop Enzo Baldini in the groin. As the policeman hit the floor, he let off a rapid burst of machinegun fire and fifteen bullets hit Gigi. He would not survive.

Malatesta was arrested after a chase. In the vehicle the police found ski masks and assumed that the trio were about to commit a cash-in-transit robbery, or kidnap a scion of one of the three wealthy industrialist families that resided nearby. During the media outcry after the shooting, the public wanted an explanation as to how a Mafia *pentiti* and a dangerous armed robber were allowed out of prison to commit further crimes. A spokesman for the Italian prosecution service explained, "We do not find information about the Mafia from nuns."

The Final Analysis

There is no disputing that the Knightsbridge Safe Deposit Centre Robbery was meticulously planned and executed. Anyone who can research, survey, organise and successfully carry out a robbery where thieves are able to spend two or more hours inside a secure vault and steal close to £40-£60 million in untraceable cash, jewellery and other valuable assets, and then to walk away with it, deserves acclaim.

Valerio 'Gigi' Viccei will go down in criminal history as an audacious and intrepid master villain, who single-mindedly spotted a rare weakness in the security set-up of a major cash depository. He possessed and exhibited all the leadership skills, confidence and arrogance that one would expect from a top military strategist. 'The Wolf', as he was known in his native Italy, was a born and bred front-runner who put his plans into practice and was willing to stand or fall by them.

If there was one serious fault, it was that the Knightsbridge robbery was committed by one professional and a bunch of grade-A amateurs. The focus was solely on escaping with the proceeds, not on avoiding suspicion or detection. As soon as Gigi and his gang set foot outside that safe deposit centre, it was a race against the clock. Gigi knew it and made a fabulous head start, but he blew it. He could have ferreted away his considerable riches and disappeared anywhere in the world, having no reason to stay and no allegiance to this country.

Once his name was in the frame, through the bloodstained fingerprint found inside the vault, the wolves of Scotland Yard came howling to his door. The cumulative effect of the crucial fingerprint, the one hundred and thirty calls he made to Parvez Latif before the raid, the paper trail that led back to the getaway van, the lack of substance shown by the inside man and some of the other gang, dictated that this crime was destined to fail. As Gigi once mused, "The rule of this game is that if they don't catch you, you are a genius. But if they do you are a miserable nobody."

I would not stoop so low as to call Gigi "a miserable nobody", but when he gave his time to lowlife like his estranged wife-cum-police-informant, he should have known his days were numbered. As the old saying goes, "If you lie down with dogs, you are bound to catch fleas," and his fraternising with a high-ranking detective and a supergrass like Malatesta only serve to compound that.

So was Gigi a modern-day master criminal or an inept blunderer, an accomplished armed robber or a professional playboy, an erring son of high society or a "romantic lunatic"? I will leave you to decide.

THE MILLENNIUM DOME ROBBERY

7 NOVEMBER 2000

Ambition is a laudable human trait. There is nothing I like more than a progressive entrepreneur or criminal coming up with a beautiful plan, and to watch it come to fruition. When I escaped from prison in 1984, I spent some of my two years at large as a fugitive living amongst the obscenely wealthy residents of the London Borough of Kensington and Chelsea. I used to derive enormous pleasure watching the denizens of this marvellous area flaunt their prosperity and possessions, as it engendered in me a raw hunger for affluence and success.

I did not want to unlawfully seize what these people possessed, as some might expect; I wanted to get out there, in our cash-laden capital, and steal the contents of security vans, which I viewed as fair game. I was, in short, driven by an unholy ambition to be resourceful and become rich. I felt, at that time, that it was the golden path to happiness. I was wrong, however, for as we shall see, ambition is not always accompanied by champagne and caviar. It can also lead to pain and perdition.

In early September 1996, a particularly compelling form of ambition was coursing through the veins of several armed robbers as they ambushed a security van in Highbridge Road, Barking, Essex. The Security Express van had returned at 9pm from another depot in Swanley, Kent, with £2 million on board, when it was waylaid at the entrance of the local depot. As a cunning precaution, the raiders drove a forty-foot, high-sided articulated lorry across the entrance of the industrial estate, which prevented other motorists and emergency services from seeing or reaching the scene of the crime.

The masked raiders then forced the three terrified security guards at gunpoint to pass out all the sacks of cash, which were placed into two green plastic wheelie bins and transferred into a stolen blue Renault van. The vehicle was then driven to the nearby steps of a Tesco store car park where the robbers changed vehicles. Police later recovered the white Scammell unit and trailer, a blue Renault van and a Land Rover with its engine still running. Forensic tests were being carried out on the vehicles while the police were hunting the four gunmen, aged between thirty and forty years old.

A Flying Squad spokesman said, "It is obviously not the first time these men have carried out a heist like this as the robbery was carried out very professionally, but it is hard to tell whether they are part of a London-wide gang."

As far as I am aware, no one was ever arrested, charged and convicted of this offence. But that is not to say that the Flying Squad never had their suspicions. All they could do – as always, in these circumstances – was to wait for a similar robbery to occur, and compare and contrast the evidence.

It would be a long wait. Almost three and half years later, at 6:45 on a cold and dark February 2000 morning, a similar gang of armed robbers ambushed a truck containing £10 million as it left the Securicor headquarters in Nine Elms, near to the famous Battersea Dogs Home on the south side of the Thames.

As the security truck left the depot and pulled into Kirtling Street, a gang of approximately nine robbers swung into action and boxed in the security vehicle with a wide variety of stolen cars, vans and articulated lorries. While a BMW car and flatbed lorry sandwiched the Securicor truck in the desolate side street, three other articulated vehicles were jack-knifed across a nearby dual carriageway in order to prevent access to the dramatic scene of the crime.

Once the security truck had been immobilised by cutting the brake lines under the vehicle, one gang member ran to a flat-bed lorry which had been fitted with a formidable iron-girder and spike. The plan was to reverse the protruding spike into the rear doors of the security truck and bore a hole large enough to retrieve the cash bags inside. But an irate motorist, who had returned to his vehicle prior to the raid, found his vehicle blocked in and removed the ignition keys from the robbers' ramming vehicle. As one robber frantically searched his pockets for the missing keys, he looked at the others in amazement at such a blunder.

Time is the currency of all armed robbers. Most professionals prepare and organise their crimes in such a way that they have enough time to escape from the venue. Hence the Nine Elms robbers' use of articulated lorries to buy valuable time, to gain access to the security truck and flee from the crime.

Alternatively, as time ticks away at the scene of the crime, the fear of capture and imprisonment for umpteen years becomes more palpable. Therefore, although the object of the robbery is to steal money, time is the most valuable commodity to the professional robber. Success or failure depends upon it.

As for the robbers at Nine Elms, the inexplicable loss of the ramming vehicle's ignition keys meant that the robbery had to be aborted. The gang set fire to several vehicles and fled through the derelict Battersea Power Station, to a wharf where a powerful dinghy was waiting to take them across the river to Chelsea harbour. There the gang torched the craft and disappeared into the neighbouring streets.

As police vehicles rushed to the incident, they were confronted with a scene of utter chaos. The jack-knifed lorries had fulfilled their purpose, causing traffic gridlock in the area. Police forensic teams scoured for vital clues but it proved fruitless, save the word 'Gertie' painted on the girder of the ramming apparatus. The hunt for a gang of ruthless armed robbers with a sense of humour was underway. But for the Flying Squad, it was back to the waiting game.

As for the robbers, one can imagine that, back at base, there were mixed emotions. Whoever was responsible for parking and driving the ramming lorry had ruined a viable plan to steal £10 million. He would shoulder the blame, and whether or not the gang would 'park him up' depended upon his role and status in the group.

Admittedly, all robbers can make mistakes, but one of such magnitude rendered the whole exercise utterly futile. The time, effort, risk and financial cost of the robbery had all been wasted. The robbers were efficient at stopping a security van on a public road, and their escape route was effective. But the formidable girder and spike mechanism was neither tried nor tested. The gang would have to commit another robbery in order to see if 'Gertie' was a real woman of substance or just another *femme fatale*, luring them into dangerously compromising situations for nothing.

The use of a fearsome ramming apparatus to acquire access to security vans is nothing new. The first one I can recall was in the early 1980s, when a gang of southeast London robbers – namely the legendary Billy Tobin, Ronnie Cook, Kevin Brown, Mark Hogg, Steve Jackson, et al – used a mobile 'Iron Fairy' crane to ram the back doors of a Brinks Mat security truck in Dulwich, southwest London. Alas, the raid was unsuccessful, as an informant (now deceased) notified the local Flying Squad and the gang were arrested in a police trap. All of them stood trial at the Old Bailey and were convicted – save one, who was acquitted because he was arrested several streets away from the robbery.

Another similar robbery occurred in November 1984, on a slip road to the M25 motorway near Reigate, Surrey. An ambitious gang of robbers boxed in a Brinks Mat security truck making deliveries and collections to local banks. Ingeniously, they pulled a monstrous mechanical digger on a low-loader trailer alongside the truck and began to literally rip the roof off the vehicle, as if opening a tin of sardines. The robbers were successful and escaped with a multi-thousand-pound haul.

I remember this crime well, as two days earlier I had escaped from a prison van at the same motorway junction. Surrey Police claimed via a TV bulletin that they were looking to see if there was a link between the two dramatic events. (I can confirm there were none, as I was firmly ensconced in a warm and cosy safe-house in east London at the time.)

At this time, it appeared as if every gang of seriously organised robbers was attempting to smash into the backs of security vans and seize the dough. Several professionals then close to me stopped a Brinks Mat security truck near Brentwood, Essex, in 1985 and rammed it with an Iron

Fairy. 'The Great Crane Robbers', as they were dubbed in the media, crashed into the rear of the security vehicle and stole £500,000 in cash.

The gang fled the scene in a stolen Range Rover and drove across fields to the changeover vehicles. By now the police dragnet was closing in, and two alleged robbers were arrested several miles away in Chadwell Heath. The police recovered the money from a nearby stolen Bedford camper van.

At their trial at the Central Criminal Court, Johnny Read and Peter Mitchell were convicted and sentenced to twenty-two years' imprisonment. Once again, *time* spent at the scene of a robbery retrieving the cash appears to be the all-important factor. Unlike the swift snatch of a cash bag or box from a security guard on the pavement, where the robbery is fluid, the crash-bang robbers remained at the scene for longer periods and took greater risks in order to go for larger amounts of cash.

More recently, however, in November 2004, a gang of professionals used an adapted JCB digger to ram the rear of a Securitas security truck in Warrington. They were successful in entering the truck and escaping with close to £1 million, but, once inside, they were hampered by the money being locked inside padlocked cages. Yet again, time was the crucial factor.

The Nine Elms robbers were still full of ambition and determination, and were up for another attempt. Their target was a Securicor truck carrying £8.7 million from its depot in Aylesford, Kent. The plan was to box in the security vehicle, cut the brake lines to immobilise it, use chainsaws at the rear of the truck to cut free the tailgate (which acts as added protection to the rear of the vehicle), ram the rear doors using another huge metal spike attached to a girder, insert an anchor-like device attached to a chain and rip the doors off of the vehicle.

On a bright and sunny July morning in 2000, they were lying in wait. As the Securicor target vehicle left the depot at 7:45am, the masked robbers sprung into action. In true professional fashion, they boxed in and immobilised the truck using a Ford Transit van and commercial vehicles. As one robber ran to the front of the vehicle, he could see the driver frantically trying to select the gears of the powerful diesel engine, and a second guard in the passenger seat putting out a May Day emergency signal on the radio. The race against the clock had already started. The robber showed the terrified guards a limpet-type explosion device with a red light flashing; he mouthed the word, "Boom!" and stuck the magnetic device to the cab of the security truck.

Meanwhile at the rear of the truck, two robbers armed with petrol-driven chainsaws were hard at work on the tailgate. They were cutting away at the locking mechanism but making little headway as they were showered with sparks. Then the seven-ton lorry with the fearsome metal spike was lined up for action. The robber driving the lorry, christened 'Gertie II', pushed the accelerator to the floor and reversed at speed into the stranded security truck. The spike made a direct hit into the vulnerable upper section which was unprotected by the tailgate. It breached the rear doors, but another run-up was needed. As the driver pulled Gertie II forward, up rose her skirt as she reversed at speed, making another direct hit. At last Gertie had done her stuff and the robbers were inside, but time was not on their side.

While the robbers were attacking the security truck, the telephone switchboard at Kent Police Headquarters was bombarded with emergency calls from workers and motorists on the industrial estate. And on the summer morning breeze, the robbers could hear the distant siren of a solitary emergency vehicle getting closer and closer.

Despite being able to see the £8.7 million in the rear of the Securicor truck, once again they had to abort the robbery. It was a bitter blow, especially after Gertie had proven herself so reliable. The robbers fled down a side street to a brown and white speedboat moored on the River Medway. The boat powered along the river for two miles, until it was dumped at New Hythe. Here the robbers jumped into their changeover vehicles and disappeared into the Kent countryside.

Back at the scene, once the security guard realised that the robbers had fled, they got out of their truck and ran along the road to safety. They told the first policeman on site, a traffic cop, that there was a bomb attached to the security truck. Immediately, the policeman ordered all onlookers and motorists to evacuate the area. A cordon was established and a call dispatched to the Bomb Disposal Squad, based at RAF Folkestone. When the bomb squad arrived, a solitary disposal expert approached the security truck with the utmost caution. Dressed from top to toe in protective apparel, he examined the limpet-like bomb and detached it from the vehicle. On closer examination, he realised that the bomb was a hoax; it was, in fact, an empty Fray Bentos steak and kidney pie tin which had been painted green and fitted with battery-operated lights.

Once again, the robbers had to abort because of the lack of sufficient time to enter and empty the security vehicle. Either the gang were not quick enough in ramming the truck, the ramming method of entry was archaic, or they had left the scene of the raid too early.

Under close analysis, several aspects strike me as bizarre. Firstly, what is the point of using bogus bombs in the cab of the truck? Did the robbers want the custodians of the vehicle to alight from the cab and assist them with entry into the rear? If that was the case, they should have used a more effective mechanism.

Secondly, while the robbers were wasting precious time, attempting to cut the tailgate using chainsaws and sticking bogus bombs to the vehicle, Gertie could have concluded her ramming duties and the robbers could have been inside the rear of the truck, chucking out the money.

Finally, although the gang had cleverly used an articulated unit and trailer to block off access to the scene of the robbery, a cursory glance at a good map would have revealed that Kent Traffic Police Headquarters was a mere half a mile away, at Junction 5 of the M20 motorway. Little wonder that a traffic policeman was first at the scene of the crime.

Many of the police vehicles seen on the motorways today are in fact intended for armed response, deployed along main motorway routes specifically to attend major incidents like the Aylesford robbery. Despite the ingenious water-borne escape route, it seems neither sensible nor practical to attempt a robbery at the Aylesford location, knowing time was going to be in short supply.

Similarly, as an active armed robber in the mid-1980s I was a member of a very successful team of blaggers, including both old and young Tommy Hole and Lenny Carter – all, alas, now sadly deceased. Just as ambitious as the Aylesford robbers, we would embrace and employ the dinosaur smash-and-grab strategy of ramming security vehicles with homemade metalwork devices. Sometimes they were successful, other times they were not and we would have to abort. Young Tommy and I were much in awe of the older, more experienced robbers like old Tommy and Lenny, and invariably deferred to their wisdom when planning a ramming robbery.

Looking back at some of the aborted or failed ramming robberies, armed with the extensive knowledge and expertise I possess now, it was obvious that some of them were destined to fail. With the Nine Elms and Aylesford attempts, we must ask ourselves whether these robbers were overambitious in their aims. As stated at the outset of this chapter, I admire ambitious people whether in the legitimate or criminal realm, but here they were, on the brink of the new millennium, using 1980s-style ramming apparatuses on modern armoured vehicles with new and improved security measures to thwart hijackers – such as mobile phone communication, data tracking and engine immobilisers. After two failed attempts, one has to question the gang's deeply flawed strategy. Success can only be gauged when you are counting the proceeds of the crime – not thinking about what went wrong.

As with all major crimes, the police put their most experienced and accomplished senior detectives on the attempted robbery at Aylesford. A quick survey of the incriminating evidence left behind revealed the robbers had painted 'Gertie II' and 'persistent aren't we' on the girder attached to the spike. Back at base, Kent's Serious Crime Squad carried out a check on the National Police Computer and established that there were startling similarities with the attempted Securicor robbery at Nine Elms, five months earlier.

Most significantly, one of the vehicles used on the attempted robbery, a Ford Transit van, had been identified by a detective investigating vehicle crime as the same van he spotted on a farm in the Kent area. Immediately, the senior detective in the case deployed specialist surveillance teams to watch and record all activity at the farm.

Tong Farm, near Tonbridge Wells in Kent, belonged to James Wenham; he had bought the farm in March 2000 for £220,000. The Wenhams were described by locals as 'the neighbours from hell', but it seemed to be a case of long-term residents resenting the fact that new blood had moved into the area. The farm was nothing special; it was a relatively untidy and rundown property with horseboxes, farm machinery and old vehicles peppering the landscape. In the recent past, the local Regional Crime Squad had shown an interest in Wenham's son, Lee, who was suspected of handling stolen goods and vehicle theft. The squad wanted to authorise fulltime surveillance on the farm, but could not justify the cost. Now their chance had come.

Due to the remote rural location, specialist police surveillance officers were reduced to hiding in flowing ditches and up trees. They noted that a former armed robber from southeast London, Terry Millman, was a frequent visitor to the farm. Millman was a well-respected old-time robber who had served fourteen years for armed robbery in the past. He was known for his permanent smile and sense of humour. Underlying his warm and pleasant exterior, however, was the dark presence of stomach cancer, for which Millman was not receiving medical treatment.

Any doubts as to whether Lee Wenham and Terry Millman had been involved at Aylesford were soon eradicated, when forensic tests ten weeks later found Wenham's DNA and Millman's fingerprints inside the Ford Transit van abandoned at the scene of the crime. Wenham's DNA was taken from discarded surgical gloves found on the dashboard, while Millman's fingerprints were found on a bucket in the rear of the van. Not confident that this evidence was enough to secure a conviction, the detectives decided to maintain surveillance and follow any visitors to the farm.

The next visitor was Ray Betson, a thirty-eight-year-old, self-confessed career criminal reared on the rough-and-ready council estates along the Walworth Road, in southeast London. As a young lad, Betson experienced the usual shortcomings associated with breadline poverty, including single parenthood and poor education through dyslexia and school truancy. Inevitably, he had learned to rely upon street wisdom as opposed to academic learning.

Like most nascent villains, Betson's criminal career started with petty theft, shoplifting, stealing vehicles and fraud. He served two eighteen-month prison sentences and climbed up the criminal ladder by cashing stolen traveller's cheques and smuggling alcohol and tobacco. Not only was Betson an intelligent villain, he was ambitious and determined. Again, like most successful criminals, Betson had aspirations to go all the way to the top of his profession. He wanted to reside in the warmer climes of Puerto Banus in Spain, where many British expats bought villas, and there was no reason why this man should not have attained his goal in life.

The beginning of his downfall, however, was when police spotted him at Tong Farm several days before the arrival of a stolen JCB digger. As each member of the alleged gang visited the farm they were given a codename. Betson was called 'bracken'.

Initially, the elite surveillance teams of Kent Constabulary believed that Betson, Millman et al were looking to attack a Securicor truck leaving a depot at Dartford. So they received the shock of their lives when they followed Lee Wenham, then Betson and his wife and children, and another potential suspect, Billy Cockran, to the Millennium Dome in Greenwich, southeast London.

Cockran, at forty-eight, was slightly older than Betson but also came from the Walworth Road, and was married with two children. A builder by trade, he was strong, reliable and unflinchingly loyal. He had previous convictions for petty crime but, like Betson, no convictions for violence.

Cockran has been dubbed Betson's second-in-command, but this is just the myth the media likes to present of quasi-military colonels and lieutenants. The truth is that theirs was a friendship based upon mutual respect. They enjoyed each other's company and shared aspirations to succeed in both lawful and criminal activities.

At the Millennium Dome, undercover detectives spotted Betson and Cockran paying particular attention to the Money Zone, where the De Beers Millennium Collection of priceless diamonds was housed. As they strolled around the venue, it's been alleged that Cockran was filming what he saw on a handheld camcorder. Inside the diamond vault, it is also alleged that Cockran even went up to the laminated glass cabinets and tapped on the doors. Later, Betson and Cockran were observed filming the perimeter of the Dome, supposedly looking for a possible escape route.

Amazingly, while Betson and Cockran were filming the Dome and its precious contents, Kent Police surveillance teams were filming them. It was almost like a scene from the impressively realistic American cops-and-robbers film, *Heat*, only this time the cops were filming the villains, unbeknownst to them, rather than the other way around.

Later that day, the surveillance team bottled Betson and Cockran at Greenwich Shopping Centre where they met another suspect, Aldo Ciarrocchi. Ciarrocchi was an unknown in police and criminal circles; a born and bred south Londoner of Italian-English stock, he was raised on a council estate, regularly attended school and was employed for a time as a casual labourer. He had one solitary criminal conviction, for shoplifting, and no form for violence.

Ciarrocchi had known Betson all his life, and had been introduced to Cockran after courting his daughter. When the relationship dissolved, Ciarrocchi met a twenty-five-year-old America model in 1988. At this time he was living in a plush Docklands flat, driving the latest Saab and aspiring to be a property developer. Despite persistent financial problems he was enjoying life, drinking at the font of happiness and pleasure. In the same mode as Betson, he was driven by an ambition to accumulate enough capital to emigrate to America and live comfortably with his beautiful girlfriend. But now he had been caught on police surveillance film, associating with his criminal companions.

The detectives assumed the meeting was something to do with the Dome, and faced an awkward dilemma when they returned to the base in Kent. They realised that the potential Securicor truck raid at Dartford was a non-runner, and that the real target was possibly the multi-million-pound haul of gemstones at Greenwich. More problematically, they also knew that a serious crime was going to be committed outside their jurisdiction, and had the unenviable task of notifying the neighbouring Metropolitan Police Force.

There were deep-seated rivalries between the Met and Kent Serious Crime Squad, as many successful south London villains had moved from the poverty-ridden council estates in Bermondsey, Rotherhithe and Lambeth to the idyllic avenues and lanes of the Kent corridor. Naturally, there was some overlap in criminal investigations, as the villains travelled back and forth to the Smoke to conduct their illegal activities. So it was always fairly arbitrary as to who would get the credit for the initial hard work of discovering that a serious crime was going to be committed. In this case, however, Kent police had little option but to share their information with the notorious Flying Squad.

The Millennium Dome project originated with John Major's Conservative government, who wanted to celebrate the onset of the new millennium in the style of the Great Exhibition of 1851. Unlike that mid-nineteenth century exhibition, which celebrated the arrival of the Industrial Revolution with all its wondrous machinery and gadgets, the Dome would be condemned as a poor imitator. Built on the derelict and contaminated land of the old gasworks at Greenwich, the massive white canopy and hundred-meter yellow support towers earned it unenviable comparisons with a female contraception device, or (at night) a beached UFO, out of fuel and out of place.

The interior space, which was the size of twelve football pitches, was subdivided into fourteen zones. Each zone focussed upon a particular theme such as the body, mind or money. The cost of the Dome grew out of all proportion when New Labour came to power in 1997, and authorised expansion in size, scope and funding. The new premier, Tony Blair, proclaimed the Dome would be "a triumph of confidence over cynicism, boldness over blandness and excellence over mediocrity". But all the British public received was a £758 million bill for a glorified tent on the south bank of the river, which could have been spent on five fully equipped hospitals.

In short, out of a projected twelve million visitors to the Dome per year, only six million actually went to the venue. The showcase celebration of the beginning of the new millennium, attended by Blair and the Queen, was a flop.

The only people happy with it were those that pocketed the money for the project, and the inveterate armed robbers from the nearby badlands of crime – Bermondsey, Rotherhithe and Canning Town – who viewed the Dome and its priceless contents as manna from heaven. Stealing the diamonds would mean swapping the traditional fare of pie, mash and liquor along the Old Kent Road for lobster and langoustines in garlic sauce along the French Riviera

The idea to showcase the Millennium Collection of priceless diamonds came from organisers at the New Millennium Experience Company, who wanted more glamour at the venue. They approached the multinational diamond conglomerate De Beers, based in London, and asked them if they wanted to promote their wares at the site. De Beers jumped at the chance and immediately donated £2 million to the Dome project, most of which was spent on the secure vault that would store the diamonds.

The *crème de la crème* of the Millennium Collection was the Millennium Star, perhaps the world's most beautiful diamond. Weighing a massive two hundred and three carats, the precious gemstone was originally found in 1992 by two impoverished diamond prospectors on the outskirts of the remote jungle town Mbuji-Mayi, in the Republic of Zaire (now the Democratic Republic of Congo). Upon discovery, the diamond weighed an incredible seven hundred and seventy-seven carats, and was quickly bought by De Beers representatives from the poor diamond pickers for £400,000. Alas within forty-eight hours of the diamond being discovered, the two diamond pickers disappeared, presumed killed by the local militia who did not receive their cut in the deal. Under tight security, the diamond was shipped to a secret location where the best diamond cutters in the world took three years to design, cut and produce the world's largest, most colourless and flawless pear-shaped diamond.

Then, at a well-publicised presentation ceremony in September 1999, held on the top floor of the De Beers Charterhouse offices in central London, the Millennium Collection was revealed to the world. As the latest James Bond movie starlet, Sophie Marceau, held the Millennium Star aloft, De Beers chairman Nicky Oppenheimer paid effusive tribute to the beauty and uniqueness of the gemstone. Like the diamond itself, the publicity was priceless for the company. The opportunity to showcase the Millennium Star and eleven other rare blue diamonds at the Dome was, like the plan to steal the gemstones, too good to miss.

When Detective Chief Superintendent Jon Shatford, based at New Scotland Yard, was told of the plan to steal the De Beers diamonds, he knew that this was his chance to go down in history as one of the great thief-takers, like Tommy Butler, Jack Slipper or Nipper Read. Shatford was an ambitious detective, who knew the value of utilising every resource the police had to apprehend and convict top-flight villains.

One of the first measures he took was to step up the surveillance on Betson and his gang. This meant not only visual surveillance, but the bugging and monitoring of vehicles, properties and telephonic communications. He even employed an innovative young civilian crime analyst, based at New Scotland Yard, whose sole function was to sit at his computer and collect, collate and analyse the open and covert evidence as it became available. By the time Shatford and the little-known Secret Investigative Services (SIS) were up and running, Betson and his gang would not be able to fart without him knowing. It really was a David-and-Goliath scenario. Betson, Cockran, Ciarrocchi and company might as well have had Sat Nav locators sewn into their clothes.

After several more visits to the Dome to assess the security and their escape route, the plan to steal the Millennium Collection began to take shape. The robbers would disguise themselves as construction workers wearing gas masks, and arrive at the Dome when the De Beers diamond vault was opened to the public at 9:30am. They viewed this as the optimum time to commit the robbery, as there would be few visitors at the vault.

The plan was to crash through an unused wire-mesh gate at the perimeter using a stolen JCB digger, enter the Dome structure through an open shutter at Gate 4 and drive right up to the vault entrance. Once at the vault, Ciarrocchi would set off smoke bombs to distract the Dome workers and the public. Betson and Cockran would enter the vault and attack the glass cabinets, using a gunpowder-powered Hilti gun which could fire specialist nails into the twenty-millimetre thick armoured glass. Betson would then attack the glass cabinets with a sledgehammer, and use bolt cutters to free the diamonds from the metal rods to which they were attached. Once the diamonds were secured, the gang would return to the JCB and drive to the nearby bank of the River Thames, where a speedboat would be waiting to whisk them away across the river to Lower Lea Crossing, where Terry Millman would be waiting in a stolen white Ford transit van to collect the robbers. After a short drive along Aspen Way, through the Limehouse Link Tunnel, the robbers could motor through the Rotherhithe Tunnel and be on home turf in less than twenty minutes.

Without doubt it was a viable plan. But what the gang failed to realise was that the Millennium Collection was frequently loaned out on tour to other diamond exhibitions around the world. When this occurred there was supposed to be a sign placed on the glass cabinets inside the vaults, explaining that the diamonds on show were replicas.

The Millennium Collection was in Paris during February 2000, Dubai in March, at Antwerp World Diamond Centre in July and Tokyo National Science Museum in September. Amazingly, it was during the September tour that Betson was observed visiting the Dome. There was no sign on the glass cabinet indicating that the diamonds were replicas. So, in theory, the robbers could have successfully stolen the diamonds and come away with a collection of worthless glass fakes.

More fundamentally, when DCS Shatford felt that there were not enough armed detectives available to man the police trap, he would order that the vault be closed to protect the diamonds. So how could the Dome robbers have known if the vault was open or not? They could have crashed into the Dome in the JCB and pulled up outside the vault to find it closed. The only answer would have been to have a spotter inside the Dome, to communicate the message that the vault was open and ready for the final assault.

Meanwhile, the Dome robbers employed the mechanical skills of Lee Wenham at Tong Farm to convert the JCB so that it could carry them all at the Dome. They also entrusted Terry Millman to purchase a speedboat for £2000. Rather humorously, he bought it in the name of 'Terry Diamond', which to a degree echoed the same sense of humour that labelled the ramming lorries Gertie I and II.

Sometime after the purchase of the speedboat, surveillance officers observed Betson, Cockran and another suspect, James Hurley, test-driving it. As far as the police were concerned, the *modus operandi* of the Dome robbery was almost identical to those attempted at Nine Elms and Aylesford, especially the use of water-borne escape routes with speedboats.

Shatford soon realised that the escape route across the Thames depended upon the high tide levels, and he could arrange the top secret operation accordingly. He knew the next highest tide was due on 6 October 2000. Several days before, surveillance teams reported significant activity around Tong Farm, where the speedboat was located, and the Old Coal Yard in Plumstead, southeast London, where the JCB was stored.

In the early hours of 6 October, a small army of police personnel congregated at the first major briefing of Operation Magician. It was held inside the Dome by DCS Shatford, who described the gang as extremely dangerous armed villains suspected of numerous high-value armed robberies in London and the surrounding counties.

In many ways, presumably for personal and operational reasons, Shatford used his persuasive communication skills to exaggerate the perceived dangerousness of the gang. For there was little kudos in calling out the big guns of New Scotland Yard to arrest a gang of negligible criminal status or importance.

Somehow, Shatford had managed to convince all those above and below him in the command chain that he required one hundred firearms officers, forty inside the Dome and another sixty positioned outside. He had another one hundred officers on surveillance and forensic duties, two police helicopters, three high-speed boats and numerous armed response vehicles at the ready. The last time armed robbers had faced such overwhelming firepower was when Ned Kelly and his gang were cornered in a remote Australian farm. It was undeniably the use of a sledgehammer to crack a walnut.

The tension began to rise, however, when surveillance teams reported the stolen white Ford Transit van towing the speedboat and the JCB at Old Coal Yard were on the move. As the speedboat was launched into the Thames on the north side of the river, another stolen Ford Transit van was chaperoning the JCB towards the Dome. Surveillance spotters, pegged out along the route from the Old Coal Yard to the Dome, reported that the JCB was making good progress until it had suddenly stopped.

Betson was contacted via walkie-talkie by Hurley and Millman at the speedboat to report that it would not start. The crestfallen Betson and Cockran had little option but to abort the raid. The JCB did a quick U-turn and drove back to Old Coal Yard in Plumstead. It had been a long and stressful day, and Shatford had to explain to his superiors at the Yard exactly what went wrong.

Shatford was concerned that, although numerous specialist SO19 firearms officers were hiding behind a purposely constructed wall near the De Beers vault, other staff and employees might notice the unusual presence of undercover police officers at the venue. He was also anxious that word could get back to the gang that something unusual was occurring at the Dome.

The problems were mounting up for Betson also. James Hurley wanted to drop out of the raid. Apparently, Hurley was not in dire need of financial resources as he owned property in Spain. More importantly, he could not wait a month for the next high tide, as he had left his heavily pregnant girlfriend in Spain and desperately wanted to get back there to fulfil his paternal duties. Hurley left for Spain during the last week of October.

Betson and Cockran began to rack their brains as to who they could recruit to drive the getaway speedboat. Preferably, they wanted someone with maritime experience. Cockran come up with Kevin Meredith, who hailed from Brighton and had gone straight into his father's charter-boat business when he left school. In 1999, he was running a fishing vessel called the *Random Harvest*, in which he would take aspiring anglers out to sea. In fact this is how he met Billy Cockran, on a fishing trip. Meredith and Cockran got along well, to the extent of the latter loaning Meredith £1400 to prop up the business.

On Saturday 5 November, Cockran drove down to Brighton Marina and asked Meredith if he would be up for a bit of action. When Meredith seemed genuinely interested, Cockran gave him the full details. He wanted him to drive a speedboat across the Thames and his fee was to be £10,000. Meredith, needing the money, accepted the offer and left immediately for London with Cockran. As the plan was to steal the diamonds from the Dome the very next day, he was given accommodation at a south London address. The gang were ready for action.

In the early hours of the next morning, Sunday 6 November, both the massive police operation and the logistical positioning of vehicles by the gang swung into action. The JCB was chaperoned from Old Coal Yard to the Dome by Betson, Cockran and Ciarrocchi, and the speedboat was about to be launched on the north side of the Thames opposite the Dome.

In the Bronze Control Room at the Dome, DCS Shatford and the Dome chairman, David James, waited with bated breath as surveillance reports started coming in about the progress of the gang. Suddenly a surveillance officer called the control room by mobile phone and stated that the JCB had stopped and made a U-turn again, heading back to the Old Coal Yard. The undercover teams were using mobile telephone communication, as covert intelligence forewarned them that the gang were using sophisticated radio transceivers to tune into police radio frequencies. Hence there was complete radio silence during the operation.

It took Shatford and his team some time to work out why the robbery had been aborted again. A quick glance at the tide timetables would have told him: the high tide on the river was not until the following day, so Meredith had aborted the raid.

With the plan put on hold for twenty-four hours, something must have been playing on the robbers' minds as, at the eleventh hour, they decided to recruit another member of the gang.

Robert Adams, then aged fifty-five, had been born in Islington and endured a hard life. He was very reserved and introspective, preferring to let others speak and to listen to them before offering anything in reply. A reputable builder by trade, Adams' speciality was as a plasterer. He had no previous convictions, save for one heart-rending domestic dispute.

Adams had been offered a lucrative contract as a plasterer to work in Saudi Arabia. He accepted it and regularly sent money home to his wife to pay the bills. Occasionally he came home for a short period, but invariably worked all the time. When the plastering contract concluded, however, he flew back to his Islington home and knocked on the door. When a friend of his answered the front door, Adams, a little perplexed, asked to speak to his wife, but the 'friend' told him he did not live there anymore. To emphasise the point, the friend pulled a blade out of his pocket. Seething with anger, the cuckolded Adams steamed into the so-called friend and stabbed him in the stomach with his own knife. He then gave his estranged wife a slap and left the premises in a daze. For hours he walked around the streets of north London, until he realised that his wife and home were all he possessed in life. Finally, he decided to surrender himself to the local police station. He was tried and convicted of attempted murder, and sentenced to six years' imprisonment.

While in prison, Adams made some new friends from the south London area. On release he would often get asked to plaster the walls of their new houses along the Kent corridor. He was sound, reliable, and needed a break. When Cockran visited Adams on the night before the raid, it was redolent of the scene in *Heat* where De Niro needs a wheelman urgently and spots a black former prison pal working in an America fast-food diner. He propositions the former robber to take part in an imminent heist. The black guy walks away from the menial job and joins the gang, only to drive into a police trap and die.

Similarly, Adams weighed up his odds, realised that there is more to life than plastering other people's properties, and decided that Lady Luck owed him a break.

But why did Betson and the gang require another recruit? The only answer (and this is still only conjecture) is that Betson was worried that someone would hop into the JCB while he was inside the vault, and either steal the ignition keys – *a la* the Nine Elms saga – or drive the digger away, leaving the robbers to make their way to the Thames on foot. Betson did not want to leave anything to chance this time.

The following morning, as the Dome robbers were preparing for a busy day ahead, so were scores of specialist surveillance and firearms officers with automatic machine pistols. Patience was wearing thin amongst the blue locus, and some were beginning to question the need for such overwhelming force to arrest a bunch of crooks with barely a firearms conviction between them. Was 7

November 2000 going to be another anticlimax, or a day of action?

As the Dome robbers prepared for the raid for the third time, the previous two occasions must have seemed like trial runs. They knew the preparation process almost by heart. While Meredith and Millman were towing the speedboat to the slipway on the north side of Old Father Thames, Betson was driving the JCB in convoy with the Ford Transit van. Inside the van were Adams, Cockran, Ciarrocchi and an unknown driver. When they reached the A102 Blackwall Approach road, it is alleged that the JCB and van pulled out of sight of the police surveillance teams, while Adams, Cockran and Ciarrocchi hopped onto the JCB for the final approach to the Dome. The unknown driver of the white van drove away from the JCB, and was never seen or traced again.

Betson made contact with Meredith in the speedboat via radio and gave him the signal, "five minutes". As the JCB drove closer and closer to the perimeter of the Dome, Betson gave the order to attack. This was the signal for Meredith to cross the Thames on the speedboat and moor the craft at the pier of the aptly-named mural, *A Slice of Reality*.

Meanwhile, Betson in the JCB had crashed through the wire-mesh gate on the perimeter and demolished the concrete bollard. He was motoring through the Dome grounds, heading for Gate 4, when he was shocked to see the perforated metal shutter that permitted access to the interior of the Dome was closed. This had never been the case before. Betson had an important decision to make, and he had to make it fast. Did he smash through the shutter, and risk flattening someone unseen on the other side, or abort for a third time?

Having ploughed through the perimeter gate and bollard, he was already too far in to turn back. Betson lined up the JCB and smashed through the shutter, sending a chilling metallic echo throughout the complex. Almost everyone inside heard the clatter as the monstrous JCB penetrated the Dome. Fortunately, no one was on the other side of the shutter as it swung around to proceed to the Money Zone and the vault. As Betson did this, he noticed two Dome workers twenty yards in front of him running out of the way of the JCB. They were not in any imminent danger, but had to move out of the way to let it pass. Betson applied the brakes to the yellow beast and stopped directly outside the De Beers vault. Adams and Cockran immediately alighted from the vehicle and ran into the vault. By now, Ciarrocchi had started igniting numerous smoke grenades to create a smokescreen for the robbers.

Deep in the Bronze Control Room, DCS Shatford and his communications team witnessed the onset of the raid on CCTV. Once the robbers had entered the vault, he broke radio silence and gave the order. The Orwellian face of modern policing sprang into action. Scores of machinegun-wielding, paramilitary storm-troopers spewed out of the gaps and crevices of the false wall. Their training had taught them to overwhelm and incapacitate their targets in a matter of seconds. Speed and the element of surprise were their watchwords. They arrested Ciarrocchi first, pinning him face down to the ground with hands cuffed behind his back. He was then searched and found to have no firearms.

Almost simultaneously, the ominous, black-garbed, armed police overwhelmed the JCB and dragged Betson to the ground, smashing his face into the concrete floor, breaking his nose instantly. As the perceived ringleader of the gang, it could almost be considered payback for the stress and anxiety caused to the firearms unit by the previous aborted raids. Face down, covered in blood, arms yanked behind his back, Betson struggled to cling onto consciousness. This was not how the clean and clinical raid on the Millennium Collection was supposed to end. This was no slice of reality, it was a surrealistic nightmare. As Betson was handcuffed and thoroughly searched, he too was found to have no firearms.

Meanwhile, inside the vault, the industrious Adams and Cockran were making great headway. Cockran had fired several nails into the armoured glass cabinets and they cracked like hardboiled eggs. With years of pent-up anger behind him and the strength of the manual labourer, Adams swung the fourteen-pound sledgehammer like a gladiator. To his utter surprise, the first blow to the cabinet penetrated the £50,000 casing. He knew that, in the next few seconds, his whole life was about to change.

A video playback in his mind promised a retirement of

sun and sea, until he heard the dreaded order, "Armed police, show me your hands!" In the distance he saw the ominous shadows entering the vault; he hit the deck as the first police stun grenade exploded, rendering both Adams and Cockran semi-conscious. Coming around as if from an anaesthetic, they found themselves physically restrained, searched and handcuffed. Latecomer Adams was having severe difficulty in breathing, as a small nasal vial of ammonia had burst open in his top coat pocket and the fumes were sucked into his lungs. A police medic was called to deal with him. Once again, both Adams and Cockran were found to possess no firearms.

On the river, Meredith had crossed the Thames and somehow moored the vessel at the wrong location – the Queen Elizabeth Pier, some hundred meters away from the agreed pick-up point. As he waited for the gang, he noticed three dark watercrafts rapidly approaching him. As they got closer he could distinguish figures in dark clothing, pointing machine pistols at him. Commonsense told him it was not the River Rescue Service. He raised his hands in the air and was talked down into the police boat, arrested, searched and handcuffed. He had no firearms.

On the north side of the Thames, Terry Millman was patiently sipping a cup of tea in the stolen white Ford Transit van. He had placed a 'NO ENTRY' road sign at the entrance of the narrow slipway, in order to stop other vehicles from blocking his escape route. When he was arrested, handcuffed and searched, he was also found to possess no firearms. All the robbers were taken to separate police stations in southeast London.

In the Bronze Control Room, both DCS Shatford and Dome chairman David James exhaled a sigh of relief, as the proactive operation came to a successful conclusion without harm to any member of the public. Shatford was especially relieved; twenty-four hours earlier he had a call from the editor of the *Sunday People* tabloid, claiming they had received an anonymous tip-off that there was to be an armed raid at the Dome. Everyone knows that journalists recruit and reward public servants – such as police or prison officers – for information that could lead to a newsworthy story, and Operation Magician was no different. In order to stem the media leak before the raid, Shatford had struck a deal with the newspaper and allowed a photojournalist to take pictures of the apprehension and arrest of the robbers.

More controversially, however, turnstile records would reveal there had been sixty-two visitors inside the Dome at the time of the raid. Among them were a group of schoolchildren from Devon, apparently annoyed that they were not allowed to witness the arrests as they ate breakfast in a nearby cafeteria. They were later joined by ninety-six Miss World contestants who were at the Dome for a photoshoot.

Disturbingly, DCS Shatford claimed that his biggest fear was for the safety of the public within the Dome.

Supposedly to prevent anyone being maimed or killed, he had amassed a small army of firearms officers to overwhelm the robbers with the utmost force. But if that were the case, why was it imperative to arrest them while they were in action, inside the Dome? Why did Shatford not give authorisation to arrest the robbers when they were on the JCB, driving up to the Dome? After all, by now there was overwhelming physical, material, visual and audio evidence to prove a conspiracy to robbery charge.

One possible answer is that he may have wanted to catch them red-handed in possession of firearms, and thus secure longer prison sentences. But Shatford could have done this by authorising a hard stop of the JCB during the run-up to the Dome, arresting them in the relative safety of the compound. At that point, if the robbers had been carrying firearms, they would have been found on their person.

Or was it merely the fact that he wanted the case to be brought home and dry, with no chance of the robbers inventing a viable defence and escaping justice?

For those who subscribe to conspiracy theories, the fact remained that there was far more publicity to be gained by arresting the robbers in action, both for the beleaguered Dome project and the De Beers enterprise.

But on a personal level, Shatford's name would be etched in the hallowed annals of Flying Squad folklore. The issue that bothers me is that he claims he was worried that the robbers would somehow find out there was a lot of police activity going on at the Dome, as he had over two hundred personnel to cover all angles of the raid. But in none of the material I have researched has there been any mention of a professional medical team on standby.

One explanation may be, of course, that Shatford was aware all along that the Dome robbers were not going to be armed during the raid. For this was the great armed robbery that never was, with the Met geared up as if to do battle with a small army.

The information could only have come from two primary sources. The first is covert listening devices planted at the robbers' homes, vehicles and other properties. The second is from an inside man, possibly even a participatory informant working with the robbers. Therefore it becomes essential to arrest the Dome robbers in action, in order to negate an acquittal should the informant be exposed as having actively set up the whole crime.

Whatever the case, Betson, Cockran, Ciarrocchi, Adams, Millman and Meredith were charged, arraigned and remanded to the top security Belmarsh Prison in southeast London. Additionally, on the same day as the Dome robbers were caught red-handed, Kent Police Serious Crime Squad raided Tong Farm. They arrested the owner, James Wenham, his son, Lee, and one other person, Wayne Taylor. All three faced various charges associated with the Dome conspiracy; more specifically, Lee Wenham was the only one charged with the attempted Securicor robbery at Aylesford.

BLAGGERS INC.

The story of a bungled attempted robbery at the Dome was a real scoop for the *Sunday People*, as the story was flashed all around the world. In Britain, the *Sun* tabloid ran the headline, 'We are only here for De Beers', while the *Guardian* broadsheet opted for 'The Great Dome Robbery'. A more sober portrayal of events made the front page of *The Daily Telegraph*: 'Police foil Smash-and-Grab on Dome's £350 million Diamonds.'

In short, the apprehension and incarceration of the robbers was a real coup for the Flying Squad, which had historically been dogged by institutional corruption and scandal. (In 1972, the head of the Flying Squad, Commander Kenneth Drury, was even jailed for seven years for accepting bungs and other favours from the porn baron James Humphreys.)

As for the deflated Dome robbers, sitting in Belmarsh, they thought things could not get any worse – until they heard, on 13 July, that their fun-loving comrade Terry Millman had yielded to the ravages of stomach cancer. Due to his fragile condition, he was being cared for in a south London hospice and had evidently passed away peacefully.

Bail for a crime of this seriousness is usually unheard of. But for those of a weaker disposition in this case – like Kevin Meredith, who could not stop talking to his captors after his arrest – it seemed a strong possibility. Meredith's solicitor had enraged the Flying Squad during formal interviews when he advised his client to shut up. But there was no stopping him, and his new allegiance was to those in authority – especially when he received bail, and took two boatloads of Belmarsh screws on fishing trips. (After an internal inquiry, seven prison officers were duly sacked.)

It was around this time, from June 2001 to May 2002, that I was also on remand in Belmarsh Prison. I had been callously set up by two informants masquerading as *bona fide* villains, who planted a submachine pistol and accessories in my car and watched me drive away into an armed police trap. I was now walking along the same landings and house-blocks as the Dome robbers. (For a fictionalised account of the set-up and how I was acquitted, read my book, *Two Strikes and You're Out!*)

I first met Ray Betson, Billy Cockran, Aldo Ciarrocchi and Bobby Adams in House Block Four. They were not very well known within criminal circles. Some of the south London villains were acquainted with Betson, but, as their prior records suggest, they were largely unknown. This is not to say that they were not popular characters, they were always approachable and willing to chat about various prison and sporting topics. Aldo was more talkative than Bob Adams, and perhaps Ray Betson was more accessible than Billy Cockran, but you could see that their main focus of attention was on their defence case. Although they did not go into their case in any great detail (if at all), the general consensus among the prison population was that they had been caught up in an elaborate police sting.

After residing for six months on House Block Four, my

security status was upgraded from standard category A to double-A (high risk). This meant I was reallocated to the High Secure Unit (HSU), basically a prison within a prison. In the HSU I was on Spur Four which contained twelve prisoners, including suspected Dome plotter Lee Wenham. Over the course of several months, I got to know Lee and found him a level-headed guy. He was polite and amiable, and I believe this was the reason he was given the job of hotplate cleaner in the HSU.

We were walking around the exercise cage one day when Lee said that, while he had been cleaning the hotplate, he was approached by the prison's Police Liaison Officer and asked to turn grass against the other Dome robbers. When the PLO was not making any headway, he changed tack and asked if Wenham would be prepared to give him any information about any of the other prisoners' cases in the HSU. Full credit to Wenham: he politely refused the offer, and came and told us on the exercise yard.

After almost a year on remand, the Dome robbers were presented at the Old Bailey for trial. They were ushered into Court Five, where they formally entered pleas of not guilty to conspiracy to rob, which carried a maximum sentence of life imprisonment – but guilty to conspiracy to steal the diamonds, which carried a maximum sentence of seven years' imprisonment. (As Shatford puts it in his own book, "The difference is that theft is the dishonest appropriation of property, and does not involve harming or the threat of injuring a person . . . convicted robbers can be sentenced for much longer terms.")

Meredith alone pleaded not guilty to both counts, on the basis that he was forced to commit the robbery by the gang.

The judge in charge of legal proceedings was His Honour Judge Michael Coombe QC – alas, the most senior judge sitting at the Old Bailey at that time. I say 'alas', as the Dome trial was to be the last case the judge would chair in a long legal career harking back to 1957. Many veteran criminals believe that, when a judge is about to retire and he is given such a high-profile, politically sensitive case, he has nothing to fear in pushing the boundaries of fairness and partiality in favour of the prosecution. Most significantly, Judge Coombe was renowned for his trenchantly conservative views and values, and would often complain in court that he was not permitted to send criminals down with much longer sentences.

In the prosecution's corner was the renowned Treasury Counsel Martin Heslop QC, who has been described as amongst the super league of prosecutors, with an incredible grasp of detail. His specialities lay in terrorism, murder, organised crime and international drug smuggling cases, although he occasionally ventured into corporate law.

The main defence counsel was Oliver Blunt QC, another leading silk who has been described as "frighteningly clever" and "at ease with any case of whatever complexity or seriousness".

In the prosecution's opening speech, Heslop threw down the gauntlet. He insisted that this was no ordinary robbery, but a meticulously planned and executed crime that utilised sophisticated machinery: "had it succeeded, it would have ranked the biggest robbery in the world in terms of value." He added that the gang were playing for very high stakes and that the conspiracy was so well organised that, if it were not for the professional diligence and expertise of the police, they would have got away scot-free with the priceless diamonds.

The most important aspect of the case, however, was not *whether* the defendants had committed the crime, but *how* they committed the crime. The prosecuted claimed it was a *bona fide* robbery, where fear and terror were essential tools, whereas the defence case was that, as no weapons or violence were used, it was a straightforward case of conspiracy to steal.

Moreover, a second arrow in the defence's quiver was the argument that the gang had been set up by a serving police officer (Betson's brother-in-law), in conjunction with a former Group 4 security guard called Tony, who had been sacked from the Dome complex some months before the raid.

Basically, the story went like this: Betson's partner, Susan, had a sister named Helen, who was married to a policeman called PC Michael Waring. The Betsons' and the Warings' paths would frequently cross at extended family functions. Waring was aware that Betson had earned his living from crime, and had submitted a memorandum to police intelligence to that effect. However, Waring tagged along with Betson while secretly wanting to bring the flamboyant criminal down.

At a family birthday party in May 2000, Betson alleged that Waring had told him he was unhappy at work, where he had recently been demoted from the CID to uniform duties. Betson claimed he asked Waring to retire from the police force to seek employment with a cash-in-transit security company, so that Betson could rob him. Waring admitted he was approached, and spoke to his wife about it. Sensing a long-term family conflict, Helen asked Waring not to report Betson to his superiors and to let the matter die a natural death. Waring agreed to it, but sometime later reported the approach to police intelligence.

Betson claimed the matter developed further when Waring said he had been delegated to guard the perimeter of the Dome, which was in fact true. Betson also said that Waring had a corrupt security guard at the Dome called Tony, who claimed that the private security at the Dome complex was crap, and had worked out a plan to steal the Millennium Star and its satellite diamonds.

In his evidence, Waring categorically denied all knowledge of this. Betson claimed that he met up with Tony at a pie and mash shop, and later at a library in south London, where Tony produced maps of the Dome complex and outlined the security procedures for the protection of the De Beers vault and diamonds. Allegedly,

Tony said that the Group 4 security guards were not authorised to intervene in any serious incident, such as a robbery, but were to monitor the situation and direct the police to the location of the crime. As a result, this would provide any criminal gang with enough time to snatch the diamonds and escape before the police arrived. It would also remove the necessity of firearms, as most of the security guards at the Dome were old and ineffectual.

To summarise, Betson claimed Waring had approached him about robbing the Dome, and had introduced him to the disgruntled Group 4 security guard, Tony, who wanted to participate in the raid but not in a prominent role. Betson's counsel argued that this was a classic situation of a serving policeman introducing an undercover infiltrator, or *agent provocateur*, to encourage others to commit a serious crime.

Betson's argument was given added weight when he claimed Tony was the person driving the stolen white Ford Transit van in convoy with the JCB to the Dome complex, which the police conveniently allowed to disappear from their radar forever. The mysterious Tony and the Ford Transit were never traced.

The prosecution countered that this was all nonsense, and that Betson had simply gone to his prison cell and written up his defence to suit the evidence. Heslop added that PC Waring had a blemish-free record and had been commended for bravery; further, he had reported Betson's approach to his superiors, and acted with honesty and integrity throughout. On the other hand, Betson was a self-confessed career criminal with convictions for dishonesty and fraud.

Predictably, when DCS Shatford was in the witness box under cross-examination, he simply refused to be drawn on the question of informants, neither confirming nor denying that there actually were any. This should have been like a red rag to a bull for the defence teams, because I believe this is where the truth about the Dome robbery is located. From experience, I know that prosecution counsel, with the support of the judge, is always loath to allow the defence to tread in such sensitive waters unless it is in the public interest to reveal this information. One of the instances in which a judge might permit such a disclosure is when it would categorically prove the defendant's innocence, preventing a miscarriage of justice.

Unfortunately for the Dome robbers, they already had one foot in the prison cell. They had pleaded guilty to conspiracy to steal, so, in order to produce such sensitive material, the defence would have had to argue that it was truly revelatory. The judge and prosecution had all the cards, and were not about to deal a winning hand to the defence.

The prosecution sensed that the only way to win the case was to establish that the robbers had created an appreciable amount of fear and terror inside the Dome. They focused upon the body armour and gas masks worn by the robbers, also on the Hilti gun, smoke grenades, ammonia and, bizarrely, a Catherine wheel found in their possession upon arrest.

The prosecution argued that the Hilti gun was a weapon, because it was capable of firing nails into concrete via the use of gunpowder. The defence successfully argued the tool was never designed, despite its name, to be used as a gun.

As for the small vials of ammonia found on Adams, Cockran and Ciarrocchi, the defence claimed these were to be used to spray the glass cabinets after the robbers had secured the diamonds, in order to destroy any traces of DNA left behind. The judge confirmed that ammonia could remove DNA, but the prosecution called an expert witness who confirmed it could also be used as a ruthless instrument of assault. Both sides agreed that the ammonia was never produced during the robbery.

More contentious was the use of smoke grenades and stink bombs. The defence claimed these were used as a distracting device and as a smokescreen. But an expert witness testified that, if the smoke was inhaled, it was toxic and could pose a risk to those with asthma or other respiratory illnesses, especially within a confined space. The defence countered that the Dome was far from a confined space, as it was capable of holding eighteen thousand double-decker buses.

The *coup de grace* in the prosecution's case came via an independent witness who said that, if anyone had been behind the metal shutter when the JCB smashed through it, they would have been killed. Members of the public testified that the JCB looked like it was out of control, and that it was chasing them. In essence, the case was slipping away from the defendants, and Kevin Meredith did not help matters when he said Billy Cockran had threatened him, his wife and family to make him take part in the robbery under duress. This bolstered the prosecution's case that the robbers were capable of viciousness and violence. The fact that neither Betson, Cockran nor Ciarrocchi had one conviction for violence between them (while Adams had a sole conviction for domestic violence) would ultimately not carry much weight.

At this stage in the trial, early February 2001, I was in the HSU at Belmarsh and Ray Betson was held in the cell beneath mine. He would come back from court in the early evening and give the lads the latest update, talking through the cell window. I distinctly remember one occasion when he told us the judge had fallen asleep during counsel's closing speeches, and was actually snoring. He said there were possible grounds of appeal in the case of a conviction, as the judge may have missed part of the evidence.

The judge was not so somnolent during his summing up, however, when he reiterated the fear and terror the witnesses endured as the JCB crashed into the Dome. He also diminished the idea of a conspiracy between PC Waring and Tony, the security guard, when he asked the jury what they could possibly gain from setting up the Dome robbers. One can imagine the defendants sitting in the dock, their minds screaming: what about financial rewards; promotion; job satisfaction; or *carte blanche* to commit crime without fear of retribution?

After sitting through nearly three months of legal arguments and evidence, the jury were despatched to consider their verdict. Seven days later, the judge said that he would accept a majority verdict. They returned a short while later with a ten-to-two majority, and found all the defendants guilty of conspiracy to rob, save Meredith, who was found guilty of conspiracy to steal. The jury must have believed his insipid argument that he was aware that he was committing a crime, but was not aware that it was a robbery.

On 18 February 2002, His Honour Justice Coombe asked for the defendants to be brought up from the court cells for sentencing. He admonished, "A value was placed on the diamonds of some £200 million. You played for very high stakes and you must have known perfectly well what the penalty would be if your enterprise did not succeed." As for PC Waring's alleged role in the robbery, he added, "as far as I was concerned it was quite apparent that he played no part in it."

The judge continued, "this was a wicked plan, a professional plan, and one which was carried out with the most minute attention to detail."

He sentenced Ray Betson and Billy Cockran to eighteen

years' imprisonment, Aldo Ciarrocchi and Bob Adams to fifteen. When sentencing Kevin Meredith, he commented, "I think in all my years at the Bar and the Bench, I have never heard a defence of duress with less merit or less substance." He sent him down for five years.

Taking into account the need for the judiciary to pass a deterrent sentence, the worldwide publicity that the trial had received had pushed the sentences way beyond what would be considered commensurate to the crime. Eighteen years for a robbery without firearms, where no one was injured or killed, made a mockery of contemporary sentencing policy and acted as little or no disincentive to robbers actually carrying firearms. One wonders whether the judge was aware of DCS Shatford's ardent belief that the Dome robbers were not bungling amateurs, but had been responsible for the attempted raids on cash-in-transit vehicles in Barking, Nine Elms and Aylesford. (In fact, the judge was sure to have seen material relating to these crimes during pre-trial Public Immunity Interest hearings.)

In order not to prejudice the first Dome trial, James and Lee Wenham and Wayne Taylor were tried separately. The cases against James Wenham and Taylor were quickly dismissed, due to insufficient and unsatisfactory evidence. The only evidence against Taylor was that he had visited the Dome on 22 September 2000.

As for Lee Wenham, he was accused of playing a significant part in the preparation of the attempted Aylesford robbery, where his DNA was found in an abandoned vehicle, and the reconnaissance of the Dome robbery, which he had undertaken while under police surveillance. Lee was sentenced to nine years for the Aylesford offence and four years for the Dome, to run concurrently.

The Flying Squad refused to let go, travelling to the Costa del Sol in Spain to track down James Hurley. In a joint Anglo-Spanish police operation, he was arrested in Marbella in May 2001. He appeared before a Spanish court and was remanded in custody to await extradition to Britain. In order to secure extradition, British prosecutors had to assure the court there was sufficient evidence to bring a charge that could possibly conclude in conviction. However, days after the conviction and sentencing of the Dome robbers, the extradition process against Hurley collapsed. After nine months in custody, he was released.

Sadly, before the Dome robbers were able to have their appeal against conviction and sentence heard, Bob Adams, aged sixty, died from a massive heart attack in Full Sutton Prison, York. Bob was a man of few words, but is believed to have said, when he was initially arrested at the Dome, "I was twelve inches away from pay day."

But little did he know that, twenty-four hours before the raid, De Beers, the owners of the precious diamonds, had replaced the gemstones with replicas. All the robbers were trying to steal were fakes. Operation Magician was a massive exercise in illusion. A robbery without any spoils; an armed robbery without guns; an accomplice and stolen van that vanished while being watched by the police, and a getaway driver who did not know he was on a robbery. Bewilderingly, this case produces far more questions than it answers.

On Wednesday 22 January 2004, at the Royal Courts of Justice in the Strand, the Dome robbers' appeal against conviction and sentence got underway. Betson had prepared a comprehensive forty-page document delineating numerous points of law on which the appeal should be based. Some of these were predicated upon the adverse effects of pre-trial publicity, whether it was ever a robbery at all (due to the diamonds being fakes), the judge falling asleep during the trial, and the pertinent fact that the robbers were unarmed and therefore deserved a reduction in their prison sentences.

Regarding the main grounds for appeal against conviction, Mr Edmund Romilly QC argued that several witnesses had observed the judge nodding off and making snoring noises, sending out the message that he had a dim view of the defence case and distracting the attention away from court proceedings. Mr Romilly added this was prejudicial to the defendants, and at the very least the conviction should be quashed and a retrial ordered. In dismissing the appeal against conviction, Lord Justice Rose cited that, although the judge had admitted falling asleep, it was only for a short period of time and during the closing speeches. He added that the trial had lasted three months, and during that time the judge was clearly awake and alert. More critically, he accused those in court of failing to wake the judge but still bringing it to the court's attention, thus hoping to have it both ways at the Court of Appeal.

With regard to the appeal against sentence, the three Court of Appeal judges said that, despite the JCB being described as a 'tank', and police officers stating that they were in fear of their lives, the absence of firearms gave powerful grounds for appeal. Lord Justice Rose ruled that the original sentences were excessive, reducing Betson and Cockran's sentences from eighteen to fifteen years, and Ciarrocchi's sentence from fifteen to twelve.

In spite of the appellants having valid and compelling grounds for a retrial, due to the judge falling asleep, it was highly unlikely that the Court of Appeal were going to quash the convictions when the trial was not, *de facto*, about the defendants' guilt or innocence. They had already pleaded guilty to conspiracy to steal, so it was about the *degree* of guilt they exhibited. (Were the raiders ruthless armed robbers or shrewd, non-violent thieves?) If the appeal against conviction had been successful, it would have been a huge embarrassment to British justice after spending £3.5 million to convict the robbers.

As the Dome robbers pondered events in their prison cells, they must have wondered how on earth the police got on their trail. In cockney villain parlance, how did this bit of work come on top?

The most logical explanation comes from the chronological sequence of events related in this chapter: the Kent detective spotted a Ford Transit van at Tong Farm, which was later found abandoned at the attempted Aylesford robbery. This led the police to set up surveillance of the farm, leading in turn to Betson, Wenham, Millman and company.

Or was it the close relationship between the sisters Susan and Helen? They spoke about the earlier visit to the Dome and were overheard by the latter's husband, PC Waring, who explicitly went against the wishes of his wife in reporting the information to his superiors.

Or was Kevin Meredith the key player in all this? He had been pulled in by the police over the attempted Nine Elms raid and was released without charge or bail. Moreover, as soon as he was arrested he was overly cooperative with his captors. Miraculously, he also received bail, unheard of in criminal circles for any sound guy. (On the other hand, getaway drivers are invariably allowed to get away if they are working with the police.) But Meredith had been arrested at the scene of the Dome raid, and later convicted and sentenced. The sentence, I have to say, would have been shorter than five years if he had been working with the police at that time.

Then there is the mysterious white van driver in convoy with the JCB, who did get away and was never traced. Was he the elusive Tony, the former Group 4 security guard, a possible police infiltrator, or an authentic friend of the robbers who fortuitously slipped the police net?

I believe we can exonerate James Hurley from any form of grassing, as the Flying Squad would not have chased him all the way to Spain and applied for his extradition, flinging him in a Spanish jail for nine months, if he was working for them. If that was the case, they would simply have left him alone.

This leaves us with the young, enthusiastic civilian crime analyst working for SO11, Scotland Yard's intelligence branch. It is alleged that he compared all the data from the two unsuccessful cash-in-transit Securicor robberies, including open and covert sources, and identified a group of individuals likely to be responsible for all the crimes. He has been described as one of the unsung heroes of modern policing, and was commended along with other covert intelligence gatherers on the investigation.

Admittedly, I would not like to pinpoint one definitive reason for the downfall of the Dome robbers. It could be the result of one of the above, or a cumulative effect of several of them, or even something else not covered here. But there is a compelling caveat for any active criminals reading this book.

When the covert intelligence cabal of Scotland Yard are on your case, pack your ambition and your tools away and go get a legitimate job, because, by hook or by crook, they will nab you.